FOR THE SENDER
Love Letters from Vietnam

music ⟵

words ⟶

Also by Alex Woodard

FOR THE SENDER
Four Letters. Twelve Songs. One Story.

FOR THE SENDER
Love Is (Not a Feeling)

*The above titles are available at your local bookstore,
or may be ordered by visiting:*

Hay House USA: www.hayhouse.com®
Hay House Australia: www.hayhouse.com.au
Hay House UK: www.hayhouse.co.uk
Hay House South Africa: www.hayhouse.co.za
Hay House India: www.hayhouse.co.in

FOR THE SENDER
Love Letters from Vietnam

ALEX WOODARD

HAY HOUSE, INC.
Carlsbad, California • New York City
London • Sydney • Johannesburg
Vancouver • Hong Kong • New Delhi

Published and distributed in the United States by: Hay House, Inc.:
www.hayhouse.com® • *Published and distributed in Australia by:*
Hay House Australia Pty. Ltd.: www.hayhouse.com.au • *Published and
distributed in the United Kingdom by:* Hay House UK, Ltd.: www.
hayhouse.co.uk • *Published and distributed in the Republic of South
Africa by:* Hay House SA (Pty), Ltd.: www.hayhouse.co.za • *Distributed
in Canada by:* Raincoast: www.raincoast.com • *Published in India by:*
Hay House Publishers India: www.hayhouse.co.in

Book design: Nena Anderson • *Photos courtesy of:* Alex Woodard, Jennifer
Fuller and Nena Anderson • *Illustration:* Anna Judd • *All excerpts used
with permission.*

Library of Congress Control Number: 2015942642

Hardcover ISBN: 978-1-4019-4854-2

10 9 8 7 6 5 4 3 2 1
1st edition, November 2015

Printed in the United States of America

SUSTAINABLE
FORESTRY
INITIATIVE

Certified Chain of Custody
Promoting Sustainable Forestry
www.sfiprogram.org
SFI-01268

SFI label applies to the text stock

"Let us strive to care for him who shall have borne the battle, and for his widow and his orphan."

—President Abraham Lincoln
Second Inaugural Address, March 4, 1865

This book is dedicated to the grandfather
I never knew, his comrades who serve to protect
our freedom, and the loved ones left behind.

And to Wayne.

Forty million veterans have served in the United States military since 1776.

Twenty-two million of them are still alive.

As high as a third of military veterans since the Vietnam War are believed at some point to experience post-traumatic stress disorder. Numbers are difficult to estimate because diagnosis and acceptance are still in relative infancy, but about half never seek treatment. Three hundred thousand cases of post-traumatic stress disorder are expected among the first 1.6 million Americans deployed to the Middle East in this century.

Twenty-two veterans kill themselves each day and in 2012 more soldiers died by their own hand than in combat.

Contents

FOREWORD

I'm going to tell you a true story that no one has heard until now besides my living room walls, a woman named Jennifer, and a worn character made of torn cardboard that holds love letters from Vietnam.

There are always stories within the story, and this tale is no different. This is a soldier's story within a father's story within a daughter's story, all within a story of discovery. I've changed no names, and names already in the public record have remained so, but in the interest of simplicity and privacy some people in the narrative will be known only by my moments shared with them. Which in the end is all that really matters anyway.

But first, Jennifer wants to share a few words with you.

One of the greatest gifts of my lifetime arrived today. I white-knuckled myself home through the snow-covered streets. I couldn't wait to open the manuscript and when I did, I read only the first few lines and then

1

scrolled down. Bracing myself. My heart pumped hard in my chest. I paused in a place or two, and the overwhelming feelings created waves in my body.

I found my way to the recliner and it began. Love Letters from Vietnam.

I was catapulted into a story. A story that is mine. My father's. But it is so much more that I could hardly keep up with the layers the manuscript took me through. I got about halfway into the book, but the waves of feelings were too much for me to take in all at once. So I slept.

My night was filled with electric dreams and I woke up at 7:00 A.M. with one thing on my mind. Vietnam.

A steaming cup of fresh coffee in my hand, the tears began to pour out of my face as I read. I hadn't cried that hard in so long, I wasn't sure how to hold my face in such a deep cry. My cat lay across my solar plexus as I read to help absorb some of my sobs, never bothered by the bouncing of my stomach or the spit that landed on her whiskers from the deep breaths blown out in between sobs.

Sobs because I was taken on one of the most beautiful literary journeys of my lifetime, and because of the impeccable timing of the delivery. I wished I could have shared what I was reading with someone close to me, but the trusted manuscript was for my eyes only. The creation before me was a book, a concert, and a movie that transcended time and space.

I finished the manuscript and needed to absorb what had just happened, so I took a walk on the snow-covered

Trinity Trails, and the pathways were illuminated with white love. It was so quiet out there, but I could hear two very recognizable notes as a song played its way through my soul: "For What It's Worth" by Buffalo Springfield. With each step the snow crunched under my feet and a mantra floated above the crisp air, almost like a prayer promising that there's something happening here.

Be ready for brilliant layers. Stories within stories that connect ever so delicately with each other.

Be ready to be taken back into history and spend time in the late 1960s.

Be ready to fall in love with animals in a new way.

Allow your heart to be cracked open by post-traumatic stress disorder and the horrors of war.

Be healed by music, as this story literally has a soundtrack with an original score.

Take a journey through devastating mountain fires, mudslides, and floods.

Be reminded of what grows after devastation.

Be prepared for your heart to fall in love with and salute the veterans you meet, including Sergeant Fuller.

Watch Alex build a house of letters with his imagination and time-travel in a way you may have never experienced before.

Be ready to explore forgiveness in way that will leave you forever changed.

And I hope that by reading this timeless book and hearing the haunting, healing, joyful, and gorgeous lyrics of the music, you will discover a message in a bottle and find out for whom the words were really written.

   With love,
   Jennifer Fuller

DA CAPO *(music)*

to play from the beginning — It., da: from, capo: head.

The guttural whisper echoes from deep in this field of burned reeds.

Vietnam.

I take slow steps against the waist-high rising water as the muck pulls at my boots and seeps in between my toes. The whisper in the reeds calls again and now I hear my name leak out through the low, hoarse spittle as I struggle to turn around because I shouldn't be walking this way, there's something here that isn't good for me, something that means to do me harm.

But the weight of this steaming humid blanket of night sky is pushing me further into the black and I fight to unseal my eyelids closed tight against the lingering searing stench of napalm. The hot breath in the reeds grows louder and louder and closer and closer until a fire of dead air brushes the back of my neck and I feel long slender fingers begin to wrap around my waist.

My eyes fly open and I sit up drenched in the gray light of dawn filtering through the bedroom window. A big brown Labrador retriever sits at attention a few feet away, assessing me with her head cocked to one side, the same way she does when I say *go for a walk* or *where's your ball* or *are you hungry*. She moves off her haunches into a braced stance and unloads a single, loud, abrasively forceful warning tinged with concern and aggression and as I pull myself out of the tangle of soaked sheets I mumble *it's okay, Stella, it's okay*.

I stumble over the same threadbare bed where her sister used to sleep and into the kitchen to make coffee before we head down to the beach, where she leaps and tumbles in the surf and shakes away the saltwater clinging to her coat. I look above her to the brushes of pink first light and see myself shaking away this saline dream, born in the secrets hidden and words unwritten that drift through the decades-old photographs and letters scattered across my kitchen counter.

These letters hold a story running deeper than the words, a story waiting in the space between the words, in all that goes unsaid, all I will never know, all I must imagine.

And dream.

WHISPER IN THE REEDS

*"One of the most painful chapters in our history was
Vietnam—most particularly, how we treated our troops
who served there. You were often blamed for a war you
didn't start, when you should have been commended for
serving your country with valor. You were sometimes blamed
for misdeeds of a few, when the honorable service of the
many should have been praised. You came home and
sometimes were denigrated, when you should have been
celebrated. It was a national shame, a disgrace that should
have never happened. And that's why here today
we resolve that it will not happen again."*

*—President Barack Obama
Vietnam Veterans Memorial Wall
Memorial Day, 2012*

The worn package with frayed seams waits patiently, mostly because when I first look inside I see a photocopied image of some impossibly colorful flower blanketing the top page. I don't possess a particularly flowery demeanor so I reflexively relegate what could be teetering toward earnest hippie bullshit to the resting place on my kitchen counter, where letters sent to me can recuperate from their long journeys. Every so often I write songs about letters and should someone want their story put to music, I'm not hard to find. I read and answer every letter, if not with a song then with a handwritten *thank you* and my thoughts about the sender's story.

And I will answer this letter with the flower, but not yet. I've found another place to live up north with my dog and horse underneath a more wild sky, the promise of open space and snow falling on pines drawing me closer to the mountains and away from the controlled chaos of this coastal metropolis. I'm only down here for a few days to pick up the last of the mail and finish emptying this house of memories and maybe get in the ocean

again before packing my truck with photographs and gui-
tars and books and heading back out on the Great Basin
Highway.

But that afternoon while I'm in the ocean, lightning
crashes in the mountains, and by nightfall the green alpine meadow pastures and gently sloping hills surrounding where I'm supposed to live are on fire. I watch from
a thousand miles away as the wind-fed flames engulf the
nearby mountains and turn toward our small valley, and
not until long after the wildfire rages through the gulch
and the water supply is restored and the melted utility
lines are repaired and any other lingering threat is quiet-
ed will the sheriff let anyone back in to see if their houses
are still standing.

So I wait.

The phone rings and the voice standing at the end of
the barricaded road up north is lost in helicopter blades
and wind, but before the call drops I can hear that one
house has already burned to the ground and the fire is
still bearing down. My helpless hands start looking for
distraction in the mail stacked on the counter, where I
find the worn package with the seal around the clasp already torn by my initially dismissive fingers. I pull out
the folds of photocopied paper with the impossibly colorful flower on top and mutter a soft *damn* to myself.

Here we go. Flowers.

But the impossibly colorful flower unexpectedly gives
way to an army-green-hued photograph of a young soldier

in fatigues, which gives way to a beautiful letter sent forty years into the past. That letter gives way to more photographs and then more letters, letters that will send me on a journey deep into the heart of a soldier, letters of love and war, service and sacrifice, annihilation and redemption, compassion and gratitude, and perhaps most of all, forgiveness.

How silly, after all these years, I still sometimes judge a book by its cover.

Sgt. John K. Fuller
366 AEMS DR. 43, Box 620
APO San Francisco 96337

Dear Sgt. Fuller,
The current year is 2008. However, I am mailing you this letter in hopes it will float back in time to 1968 to where you were then—Da Nang, Vietnam.
My name is Jennifer Fuller. You won't know me for another two years, but I am your daughter.
I know to another who may be reading this, it may seem unusual—yet I know you understand. I have been reading the letters you wrote to your wife, Rebecca, during your tour in Vietnam and I am sad I only have a small portion of them. It seems you wrote her two to three times a day.
This one I found especially sweet. I will always cherish the timeless love story of my dear parents. The letters you wrote my mother have bridged a gap in my heart and have allowed me to understand a tiny piece of the place I came from.

Honey,
I was sitting here missing the hell out of you so I just had to write. There should be a law against a woman who has a hold on a man like you have on me. I think of you every minute of the day, and the memory of your love tortures my old body all day long. On top of that, I won't accept any substitutes

for you. I came here and cut myself off, and only you can turn me on again. What I am trying to say to you is that I love you with all my body as well as my heart. (I am proud to say it too.)

Darling, when you send me my trumpet, include some valve oil in it. I am anxious to get my horn, so please rush it along. By the time you get this, I will know about Hawaii for sure. I am going to call you on the 5th, give or take a day. What a great time we are going to have on my R&R. Me and you together for six days.

Sweetie, I will close for now. By the way, I call you Rebecca (instead of Becky) because it's your real name and I think it's pretty. I love you and that name is music to my ears.

I love you too much, Rebecca.

John

I won't tell you how it all ends, for you have an entire life ahead of you. I can tell you this much: I turn out pretty good. You would be proud to know I have inherited many of your traits. Some of those traits I had no idea came from you until now. My passion came from you and it is something I will cherish from this day forward so long as I live.

I also want you to know I have all of your musical instruments in the room I'm currently writing in (your trumpet, saxophone, bass guitar). I had no idea that you played in a band during your Vietnam tour. I know you hated it there and made the best you could out of things.

I never heard you talk about this part of your life and was never even curious about it until now.

You complain a lot about how hot it is there and how Charlie is always making you run to the bunkers for cover because of the incoming rockets. (I had to look up what Charlie means and you guys apparently call the Viet Cong "Charlie.") Your son (or baby boy as you now call him) explained to me why you didn't like talking about your tour there. Everything about war is brutal and you feel it is so unfair to be away from the one you love.

I can't lie and say you didn't make a lot of mistakes in your life after you returned home. The letters you wrote to Rebecca, however, were so loving and sweet, maybe a little too steamy for your daughter to read! I learned a lot about you and I know this to be the truth: You loved three things with all your heart, for all your life—Rebecca, your kid, and your music.

I won't get into the details of what happened, but I want you to know that your wife stayed true to you. She never really loved another.

I was hoping too, that you could find a way, wherever you are, to write her one more letter. You know exactly what to say and she is still as pretty as you describe her in your letters. You have a beautiful way of writing and there is one big letter yet for her to read from you. I know you will find a way to get it to her.

It won't be long until you are with her again in Hawaii. Hang in there, soldier. This is what you have to look forward to:

Jennifer

Boy do I Love
you !!!

I let out the breath I've been holding since I read the words *I am your daughter* and my exhale pushes open the front door into a house this letter has already built in my imagination, a house where a soldier, his wife, and his child eat and talk and sleep and dream. This missive sent back in time has framed the story of a soldier's life, with timber culled from a present soon to become his past and nails driven into his future by these words of a daughter he doesn't yet know.

I close my eyes and walk through the downstairs rooms but find no bed where the soldier confesses his mistakes, no couch where he has sat with his head bowed in regret, no photographs on the wall showing me what the years ahead will bring, only this picture of a young couple on vacation with a waterfall and palm tree in the background. So I walk down the hall and turn a crystal doorknob into another room, where I find oil paintings showing historic battles I can't identify and bronze statues of heroes with names I can't place and crisp uniforms worn by soldiers in wars I know nothing about.

These are the artifacts of our wars.

But I don't recognize any of the paintings or statues or uniforms so I open my eyes with the letter and photographs still in my hands and mutter *am I that igno-rant?* I have no idea what the word *Charlie* means, except as a faint attachment to a scene from some movie that has also given me a cursory awareness of other words on the page like *Viet Cong* and even *Vietnam.* These words must still echo from the past battlefields of soldiers at war to the minefields they walk here at home, but they are words I don't understand. I doubt I could even find Viet-nam on a map without searching for several, too many, moments.

I'm brought back to the kitchen counter by the televi-sion faintly sighing the opening moments of a preseason football game. Yesterday's echoes of a local television news story about a Vietnam veteran return across the chasm of my short attention span and I think I remember something about him shooting somebody, or maybe he got shot in some maelstrom of booze or drugs or firearms or all three. There may have been something about some mental condition but I'm not sure, because I tuned out the drone of the newscaster and went about the small unimportant things that make up our very busy, very important days.

So yes, I say to the photograph I'm holding of the young soldier standing next to the ammo, *I am that ignorant.*

And acknowledging my ignorance makes me realize that I hardly know what any words from any of our wars mean because I've been so sheltered by the very freedom fought for and protected by the soldiers who said them.

So I'm ignorant *and* sheltered.

Sometimes life's timing is suspicious. The first notes of the national anthem spill from the tinny television speakers and I drop the letter on the counter for the ritual that happens every time I'm alone and football is on TV. I put my hand over my heart, like I'm in Mrs. Bryant's third-grade class again saying the Pledge of Allegiance before roll call at Lowell Elementary School.

But instead of saying the Pledge of Allegiance, I sing along under my breath to the national anthem and feel the familiar air catch in my throat. Until now I've always thought this happens because of pride, like when parents get choked up watching their kid onstage in their first big role as a bumblebee or Abraham Lincoln in the school play. And while I'm proud to be an American, just like I'd probably be proud at my hypothetical kid's first play too, the discovery of my own sheltered ignorance at the kitchen counter tells me this isn't pride making the air catch in my throat.

Because as I watch these images of men and women in uniform carrying the flag and jets flying overhead and fireworks going off and players crossing themselves, somewhere in my heart the uniforms and jets and flag and fireworks and players crossing themselves become something else.

The uniforms become those who fight, the jets become how they fight, and the fireworks become the fight. And the flag becomes the freedom they fight for, the

same freedom that allows those players to cross themselves under whatever god they choose, and for that I am
grateful, enough to almost cry during the national anthem at a football game in the sacred solitary freedom of
my living room.

That fire of gratitude, reignited by the spark of this
letter on the counter, shines a light on a certain kind of
shame I feel for not having a better understanding of
those artifacts of war. I should know deeper the words,
the motives, the people, the context, the cost.

The last *brave* of the national anthem fades away
into the upper decks of my ceiling and I sit down on the
couch next to my road-beaten guitar, born in 1969, the
year after this love letter from Vietnam. My eyes settle
on a plexiglass case in the corner of the living room and
trace the contours of the weathered trumpet inside until
they rest on the words *Liberty Model* etched into the horn.
This relic dominated a closing window in my grandfather's life between the Great Depression and World War
II, when he sang and played trumpet in Spike Jones's
swing band, before he left music to serve on a Navy warship, before his ship was sunk in a brutal surprise attack
early one December morning at Pearl Harbor, before he
was called upon in the aerial ambush's aftermath to identify his fellow soldiers by their teeth.

My dad told me that my grandfather didn't like to
talk about what he saw and felt and brought back from
World War II, that men back then didn't talk about those

things. They got jobs and buried their darkness because that's what the world expected men to do.

But the darkness can creep back up and show her face in so many ways. And sometimes if the darkness isn't enough to stop our hearts, what we do to bury her will.

As my eyes follow the mouthpiece of the trumpet back down past the slides to the bell, I draw my first line of honor between the grandfather I never knew and his military service. I never knew my grandfather as a veteran because I never knew him as a grandfather.

I only knew him as this trumpet, because his own heart stopped on the side of a California road when my dad was still a teenager.

One of my favorite photographs is of my grandfather holding my dad a few years after the attack at Pearl Harbor. There's a joyful love in the smile that the man shines onto his only son, there's playful innocence in the part combed into his son's hair. Behind them are stairs leading up to a screen door and behind the screen door is a darkness set off by the striking white of the Navy uniform.

And there are stories in the serviceman's strong hands, a living story in the shape of my dad and another story, an untold story of the weight those hands may have carried home from the war, a story that disappeared into the ether one afternoon on the side of a California road.

*

I wonder if Sergeant Fuller's trumpet looked and sounded anything like that one standing in brass salute in the corner. And I wonder if he played the horn in his band in Vietnam in some low smoke-ceilinged Da Nang club where soldiers escaped the war outside, where they went to bury the fear of their unknown and the missing of their girls back home and the bodies of their brothers.

I can't go back in time and walk into that club or onto an Air Force base or through a South Vietnamese village. But I can read and listen and learn more about the war, and how that turbulent era unfolded in the decade before I was born. And maybe for now I can somehow honor this gratitude by closing my eyes and wrapping my fingers around this old guitar and imagining myself singing from a soldier's heart.

I feel a brush along the back of my neck as I randomly play the steel strings already rusting from the salt air and one of my old songs pushes to the surface. I try to remember the words I haven't sung in over ten years, written when I was on the edge of a broken dream and looking for a way out to somewhere, anywhere other than here.

By the time I get to the second verse the lyrics are coming more easily. I sing the words *waltzing with Morrison* and over the next few chords absently wonder why I included the name of the singer of a band from the late

'60s that I never really listened to. I could see myself putting Springsteen in a song, but not Jim Morrison of the Doors.

My heart quickens and a familiar knowing edges onto the couch between the letter and my guitar. *This song wasn't written for then, it was written for now.*

The knowing will soon eclipse all doubt as I discover how much this soldier belonged in love and needed escape. And I've felt this knowing before, that a song from my past was really for my present, but I won't look at why since I would have to think about her. And I can't do that now.

Now I have to sing. Because I may know little about the artifacts of war but I can do something with what I do know. I know this song, written as my own escape years ago, so I close my eyes and imagine the distance and weight of war and now I sing from the heart of a sweaty, young, homesick soldier named Sergeant John K. Fuller who closes his own eyes and waits for his angel, his chariot to come and take him home.

*　*　*

chariot

some nights i lie awake
waiting on my angel to take me away
sometimes when i sleep
i see her face
she takes me up into the sun
where we are waltzing with morrison
this is where i belong
i belong in love

as we shoot across the stars
and my old world seems so far away
i have to close my eyes
so not to cry

way up here we can sing our song
over the places where we didn't belong
this is where we belong
we belong in love

so don't wake me now
i beg you please
don't wake me now
i'm way too deep
don't wake me now
just let me sleep

in the morning i'm awake
is this the same place as yesterday
i have to close my eyes so i can see

this is everything
everything i need
this is everything
everything i need

here i come
your chariot
here i come
coming to take you home

*   *   *

The book of letters written by John Steinbeck is open to a passage describing one of his first encounters with soldiers in Vietnam. Steinbeck was embedded with the U.S. military during the Vietnam War and I'm taking my first steps toward learning more about this war with *The Grapes of Wrath* author as my guide. His letters back home were also love letters from Vietnam, written in tribute to his beloved friend Alicia who had just passed away. Each one is addressed Dear Alicia and recounts a moment or observation or reaction while he was in Vietnam.

I look back down at the words about meeting the soldiers and read: *We loop over to a chopped out clearing so small that our rotor blades barely clear the giant bamboo. Out of the undergrowth, thicker than any I have ever seen, faces, or really only eyes, appear. Mottled helmets and fatigues disappear against the background. Faces black or white from sweat and dirt have become a sort of universal reddish gray. Only the eyes are alive and lively. And when we settle and the rotor stops, their mouths open and they are men, and what men. Can you understand the quick glow of pride one feels in just belonging to the same species as these men?*

I wish I could talk to one of these *men, and what men* he describes, one of these soldiers who could make Vietnam more visceral and personal to me, especially Vietnam in 1968 when Sergeant Fuller writes his love letters home. If I could I would ask that soldier what he has seen and still sees, what haunts him, what he comes home to, but I don't know any Vietnam veterans or know anyone who knows any Vietnam veterans. And I'm reluctant to ask around because I now have a heightened sense of respect, uncovered in these first efforts to scrape the flakes of rust off my sheltered ignorance. The more I read about the Vietnam War, the more I get the feeling that books about war, any war, are nothing like being there.

And if Sergeant Fuller doesn't talk about his time in Vietnam, why would any soldier want to talk about what is probably their darkest window, a window through which he still must look every day, a window he will never be able to turn away from in a room he will never be able to leave in a house filled with the artifacts of war.

*

Every week I bend down to pick up this community newspaper off my driveway. I keep the plastic bag for what gifts Stella may leave behind and throw the actual paper into the recycling bin, because all I think I will find inside are supermarket advertising inserts and middle-school football scores. So why I'm absently leafing through the pages today by the trashcans behind the house is a mystery.

Until I see the photograph.

The camera lens has caught a surfer, maybe in his sixties, carving a deep turn on a wave. The caption under the photograph reads *Fundraiser to be held for soul surfer and combat veteran,* and the first couple of sentences in the article give details about an upcoming benefit at a local bar to help this veteran pay for dental work that the Veterans Affairs hospital won't cover.

And I feel that same deep brush on the back of my neck that I felt when I first played Sergeant Fuller's song "Chariot" on the couch, as my eyes jump ahead a few paragraphs and land on the words *Vietnam* and *1968* and now I know why I'm holding this newspaper in my hands by the trashcans behind the house.

*

The next week I go to the benefit at the bar but I don't talk to him. I don't even see him in the crowd gathered toward the back of the room and I'm not sure what he looks like anyway since all I have to go on is that newspaper photograph. And as I sit there at the bar I wonder *what would I say? Hey, nice to meet you, tell me about hell?*

So I nurse my beer and stare straight ahead at a flyer for the fundraiser taped to the wall above the cash register and I've seen this flyer before, stapled to the telephone pole at the corner of my street. I remember a few weeks ago waiting for Stella to finish her business and looking at the homemade collage of photos and text with obliviousness disguised as a mild disinterest bordering on disdain and thinking *why does this veteran need new teeth, he looks fine, doesn't he have a job?*

And now I feel like an asshole so I pay for my beer and walk past the cover band assaulting a Tom Petty song and I leave the bar as anonymously as I arrived. No, Tom, I guess there ain't no easy way out and yes, I am backing down and I retreat across the parking lot, climb into my truck and head down Highway 101 into the starless night.

*

He tells me he was sent to Vietnam in 1968 and came home on the Fourth of July in 1969. Most of his platoon chose to pay for their own airplane tickets back to the United States so they could wear civilian clothes, since they heard they would be met at the airport by screams of *baby killers!* and batteries and rocks and whatever else could fit in angry hands.

The protestors were there when he landed anyway. They knew who he was even without his uniform and they screamed *baby killer!* at him and all sorts of other filth bolstered by the fragile strength of anonymity in groups, the same false confidence found in looters and rioters, vitriol fueled by hate directed toward this young man who was a boy before he left to fight a war he didn't choose.

I wonder silently if the same people who saluted him when he left gave him the middle finger when he came back and he says the cutting shrieks of *baby killer!* got louder and louder everywhere he went, even though he wasn't a baby killer. He wasn't one of the soldiers under orders to shoot men and women and children suspected of being Viet Cong in the horrific My Lai Massacre, which everyone at home saw on television and damned an entire military for from the comfort of their living rooms. He didn't rape any women or burn any villages and he says if he hadn't been hundreds of miles away he would have been one of the soldiers at My Lai that day standing up for the innocent and trying to do the right thing.

He says the words again and looks down at his cup of tea.

I'm not a baby killer, man.

His first night home showed him what his life would become when he heard the Independence Day firecrackers go off that sounded like mortar rounds and the whistling Piccolo Petes that sounded like incoming rockets and he fell to the floor with his head in his hands, his heart racing and panic rising and his throat unable to push around air. This Independence Day for his country would be his first Dependence Day, because he would use every street drug he could find to quiet the penetrating screams in his mind that kept him wide-eyed almost all night every night, punctuated only by the nightmares he doesn't tell me about. When he did sleep what he saw in his dreams started telling him to kill himself and the only thing that silenced the demon was a slow dance with heroin, a one-night-only waltz that would last for more than a decade.

As he looks away at the ocean into another time I remember my dad telling me that he would sometimes walk in on Vietnam veterans working in the family-business factory and they would have needles in their arms. They would look up at him and be honest and sorry but he would have to fire them because heroin and heavy machinery aren't friends, heroin is only friends with herself.

The veteran's eyes come back to me and he says when not even heroin was a friend anymore and suicide was his only solution he landed in lockdown at a psychiatric ward in Denver. He says he watched the other veterans in the hospital walking up and down the halls with *no one home*, their blank stares numbed by Thorazine and asks me if I know what Thorazine is and I say *I have a horse and I think that's a horse tranquilizer*, and he nods his head and says *well, would you take it?* He had spent enough time with *no one home* by then to know the drugs would only lay a soft blanket over the carnage so he started hiding the pills under his tongue until he could throw them out.

After the hospital wouldn't hold him any longer he spent some lost years trying to find himself, but he couldn't find much that wasn't broken. He made his way back to this stretch of coastline, where standing in front of the ocean one morning he remembered what he'd forgotten. This ocean gave him solace and peace as a child and maybe she could give that to him again.

And so he surfed every day, the waves easing his demons like no drug could. He discovered a healthier way of living and thinking in the small things and managed to hold down a job and eventually started his own small construction company so he could get in the water every day before and after work.

He looks out at the sunlight glinting off the waves a few hundred feet from where we sit and says *surfing saved my life*.

A still moment passes before he stands from the table and pulls up his shirt to show me the sections of stomach and leg and arm gnarled by over twenty VA surgeries, some of them failed procedures and most of the rest attempts to undo the failures. The first surgeries weren't done until thirty-five years after he came back from Vietnam, when his insides burst from a marriage of Agent Orange and shrapnel that had worked its way up to his colon.

Most of the shrapnel came from the night he was called back from his reconnaissance unit to secure the perimeter of a base outside Tay Ninh. He had volunteered for guard duty that night, which is the only reason he's alive today, because the Viet Cong fired a rocket that hit his bunk and would have killed him instantly had he not been on the guard tower. The second rocket blew him off the tower, forty feet down into a three-foot puddle of water that broke his fall.

He says the deep searing pain from shrapnel lodged in his intestines, broken ribs, torn meniscus and rotator cuff and triceps tendons, a fractured hip and compressed discs in his back put him in the Army hospital for a few weeks but he wasn't actually operated on until years later. Instead he was back in the field again when the Viet Cong overran his team in a firefight at a mostly underground base called Mole City. He stood on top of his bunker and called for air strikes and lobbed mortars straight up at the enemy until help arrived, but by then over two hundred of his comrades had been killed and only seventeen lived, and of those who lived only six walked out on legs not severed by searing rocket blasts or grenade explosions.

He was one of the six, but the shrapnel still lodged in his stomach would come back to almost kill him years later and continues to cut his still-bleeding insides. He says he was awarded a Bronze Star and his second Purple Heart soon after the firefight, and before the generals and majors arrived for the ceremony they had to stack the dead Viet Cong in piles so the hundreds of bodies and body parts could be torched by Cobra helicopters.

After the ceremony he couldn't escape the heinous images of the firefight and he was sent to the Army mental ward, where they told him his problem was something called chronic battle fatigue. They said his condition was treatable with pharmaceuticals so they loaded him up with antidepressants and sent him back to Tay Ninh to do supply work. He wanted to finish his tour with his reconnaissance team, so he headed back into combat and a couple of months later he was on a plane home on the Fourth of July to be met with screams of *baby killer*.

His voice trails off and I think the story is over but after a quiet pause he gives a coda to his song, a lyric that shakes as the words fall from his mouth.

I will never forget that smell of death and burning flesh. Never.

He looks at the ocean again and says *I've never gotten all the way through that story before* and then looks at me and tells me there's something about me that puts him at ease, that I somehow have more life in me than my age suggests and *how did you find me?*

I found him through the writer of the newspaper article I read by the trashcans behind the house, who told me *he's a really friendly guy, just call him* and gave me his number. But I felt like this intrusion was somehow disrespectful so I wrote to him, and when he didn't respond I did actually use the phone and now we are sitting here together steps from the ocean. I tell him what I'm doing, that I have these letters from Vietnam and I want to sing about them from the heart of the soldier who has written them and since their time in Vietnam overlaps, maybe I can sing through him too.

He doesn't say anything, he just looks down at his cup of tea and then at the ocean and then at me and then only then does he quietly murmur *wow*.

*

He and Sergeant Fuller both arrived in Vietnam in 1968 to fight the communist North Vietnamese Army and Viet Cong and Charlie because the United States feared that the spread of Communism in Vietnam would infect the region and threaten democracy's interests everywhere. They called this "the domino theory" and the

U.S. government wanted nothing to do with dominos, so at first the politicians sent soldiers not to fight but to advise the weaker, untrained anti-communist South Vietnamese Army. But a controversial moment between the North Vietnamese Army and an American warship in the Gulf of Tonkin would send the first of hundreds of thousands of soldiers to Vietnam through enlistment and the draft, in this war where success wasn't measured by enemy territory gained, but by enemy body count.

Some of the soldiers were hometown high-school quarterback heroes fresh off their senior season, some of them were from the inner-city streets, and some of them were searchers trading trouble with the law for service to their country. Some soldiers were already decorated war veterans, some soldiers were just kids who didn't finish high school and had nowhere else to go. Small towns, big towns, farm towns, no towns; they came from every-where, for all sorts of reasons, to fight an outside nemesis while the greater threat evolved amongst them, inside them, in a war that made less sense to many of them the longer they fought. But even then, they fought for each other.

Back home the climate began to change from Viet-nam War opposition at rallies and sit-ins and teach-ins and love-ins to hate directed at the soldiers. As I learn more about the war I see the hatred, even now, in anon-ymous misspelled rants all over the Internet. I have to read again a post in the comments section of a decorated

Vietnam veteran's website because the attack seems so nonsensical and misdirected: *You fought a filthy war you had no right to be there. You raped and mutilated women and babies. Yes you are baby killers!!! It was a filthy war and the legacy left behind can be summed all up with my lai and agent orange that is the recognition you deserve to claim as your own mess.*

And never have I seen clearer that the beautiful thing about the Internet is the ugly thing about the Internet, which is that it gives everyone a voice, especially those who don't want to be accountable for what they say and can hide anonymously behind pithy aliases.

The same freedom that allows anger and venom and stereotyped filth to be spewed against entire races and religions and groups of people allows me to question whether some people deserve to even have a voice. Because words like *yes, you are baby killers* are born in the same kind of one-must-be-all generalizations that fuel racism and anti-Semitism and most every other *ism* ruining humanity. And this flaw doesn't belong only to a particular country like America or one religion like Islam or a movement like the Aryan brotherhood.

This flaw of stereotype belongs to humans across recorded history, perpetuated by small people with big voices who would rather hate a face than an idea, and even smaller people who would rather hate whole groups of faces than look in the mirror.

*

The fibrous brushing of the combat veteran's calloused fingers against the paper tag on the edge of the teabag brings me back to him. This soldier who never killed a baby is part of a military tradition of fighting for the freedom of his countrymen to protest and have barbeques and watch football on Sundays. He followed his orders in service and now carries burdens no one should be expected to bear without help. I wonder if the protestors waiting for him at the airport that Fourth of July in 1969 are the same ones now hiding behind their computer screens, if maybe in the glowing glass reflection they see themselves as they looked decades ago. And if they do, I wonder if they are yelling *baby killer* and spitting and throwing batteries at him because they can see him react, they can hurt him, and they can use him as a mirror for whatever anger and hurt and disappointment they have in their own lives.

I wonder if they have discovered what beauty may be found in being for something instead of against something, as Steinbeck wonders in one of his letters from Vietnam when he writes: *I must believe that the plodding protest marchers who spend their days across from the UN and around the White House hate war. I think I have more reason than most of them to hate it. But would they enlist for medical service? They could be trained quickly and would not*

be required to kill anyone. *If they love people so much, why
are they not willing to help save them? This country is woe-
fully short of medical help.* . . . *It might be dangerous to use
this method of protest, and besides, if they left the country,
their relief checks might stop. But in return they might gain
a little pride in themselves as being for something instead of
only against.*

And I wonder if now, years later, they ever make a
distinction between the healthy and necessary freedom
found in opposing a war and the fear-driven, selfish im-
prisonment found in opposing the man.

*

He shakes his head and says he can't believe what I'm
doing with the letters and songs and that I'm shining
some light in a dark world and *I got the chills all over me,
look at that!* And he shows me the pinpoints of raised skin
on his arms and I think to myself *I know the feeling* and
then he says *I think there's something going on here, there's a
bigger reason why I'm here talking to you.*

And my gut tells me that our time talking about Vietnam is done. The names of the brothers he lost there will
stay in him, nestled somewhere between the way the hu-
midity of the jungle lay over him like a hot wet blanket on his first night in the country and the sting of the
screams that hit his cheek when he came back home.

I will only take what he has given me about his time there because by now I can feel the rest.

I ask him about his life before the war and he says he remembers himself as a carefree kid, spending his teenage years in a Beach Boys' song, running around this beach town and surfing and chasing girls and being a kid. *Just being a kid, because that's all I was.*

He pauses to drink some tea and my mind retreats to stills from a documentary my dad showed me about how my grandfather's ship saved the crew of a U.S. aircraft carrier that was bombed and sunk by a kamikaze pilot in World War II. And my dad started crying, but I don't think his tears were only for his father, because the break in his voice came strongest when he said *those soldiers were just kids, eighteen or nineteen years old, fighting for us.*

Look at them. Just kids.

*

I leave him watching the waves and get up quietly from the table to fill my coffee cup but before I sit back down he's already talking again, telling me that when he came back from the war he may have been closer to being a man but something wasn't right. He didn't talk about what he saw or did because nobody wanted to hear about what evil from Vietnam was creeping around in his heart, nobody wanted to rehash what's best forgotten, nobody cared about baby killers anyway and even if they had, men didn't talk about these things, they just did what men were supposed to do. They got over it and found jobs and had families.

But he couldn't do any of that very well.

His body was ravaged from battle but he knew this wasn't his biggest problem, that the knife still cutting through him today to undo what damage can never truly be undone would do nothing for his rebelling and fighting and screaming mind. He had left his soul on a battlefield in his past, his voice silent and buried in a time before what would become his validation was even a hyphenated group of words.

He says everything changed one afternoon after almost thirty years of fractured relationships with himself, his wives, and his kids, when a woman told him about a new diagnosis called post-traumatic stress disorder. As she talked he heard himself in her words and sensed that maybe there was a way out of here and when the woman said his wife should come with him next time, the long journey of rebuilding a man began.

I drain another cup of coffee and we talk some about his ongoing treatment, but mostly about surfing and the friends he's met in the water. And now I understand the weight and truth of what he's already told me, because while acknowledging and treating his post-traumatic stress disorder may be saving the man, through his stories of the ocean I can hear that surfing has saved the life.

He says his relationship with his kids is better than ever. His son is an accountant and his daughter is back to good again, now that her own trek into hell following the darkest of her dad's footsteps has ended. She ran away from home as a teenager and he had to hire someone to find her and pull her off the street and away from the meth and take her to a rehab center in Utah, where she could begin her life again. She found work helping returning soldiers with their addiction problems until government-funding cuts a couple of years ago took her job, but he says that she's still doing what she can to help, and that because of her work she understands him even more now.

He talks to his kids every single day and tells them he loves them and they say they love him too and this is the most beautiful thing in his life, this is his silver lining, and the last thing he tells me before he stands up from the table is *if there's one thing I know, it's that no matter what fucked-up stuff you go through, there's gonna be a silver lining somewhere down the road.*

In the parking lot is a beat-up van with surf stickers plastered on the windows and he says *this is me* and I hold out my hand and he takes my wrist and pulls me into his lean, battered, scarred body and holds me close and says *thank you for what you are doing* and then lets me go and I let him go, but not really.

Because I will carry his stories in me with a photograph moment of this man sitting across the table, this surfer staring out at the glinting waves on the ocean that has saved his life, this soldier who fought first for his country and then for his life, this veteran whose service we must honor as we would protect our last flame in a storm.

Sgt. John K. Fuller
366 AEMS DR. 43, Box 620
APO San Francisco 96337

Dear Sgt. Fuller,
You will be receiving a few more letters from the year 2008. This is your future daughter again. As I have been reading more of the letters you wrote Rebecca from Da Nang, I have also been searching through the pictures you included for her in the letters. In this one, I see you looking above the horizon of your life, toward everything that is out there waiting for you. I can see in your eyes that you are a deep thinker and a dreamer, more traits I was gifted with by you. You are a beautiful man, a dichotomy, a perfect portrait of the light and the dark. I often think I inherited your dichotomy.

Dearest Rebecca,
No mail from you today or yesterday. I hate this place even more when the mail doesn't come in. Everything has been quiet here, but we are just about due for a nice little attack. We really haven't had one with more than three or four hits since the offensive last January. Of course, I'm not lonely for the sound of bombs, but the Viet Cong like to let you know they are able to hit whenever they want. The last three months, we have kept them on the run too much for them to do anything and I hope it stays that way.

While I am on the subject of war, something happened the other day that really surprised me. A VSO tour bus blew up on the way back from a tour of Da Nang City and some of the outer villages. I guess it was a time bomb planted under the hood because nobody got killed and the only ones hurt badly were the driver and another guy seated in the front. I was about to go on one of those tours, but I had a change of heart. I will do all my sightseeing here on base where it's safer!

I thought you might like to hear one of the bad things that happen in the area, because I know you wonder about what is going on here. I am glad I hardly have anything to tell you to that end because that means nothing is happening!

Sugar, I will close for now. Be good and say. . . do you know I love you?

I do, and very much too.

John

It's all in your eyes. All the answers are there. You are not looking into a camera lens; you are looking into your future. You are looking at the image in your mind's eye of your sweet Rebecca. You are sending passion through space and time, through a click of a camera and a picture placed in an envelope.

As you paused and stared into the horizons of your life, could you have ever known your last spark of light would spread to my night sky and send me in search of meaning?

You and your journey have been the key to the lock of my soul. Your journey has inspired me to ask the hard questions. It carried me through the clouds of dark as I search for the light. I see myself in you in the above picture as your eyes stare out into the mystery of the world. I hear in your words in the above letter that you are very much aware that our story must sometimes include pain, but ultimately it's about finding the life in the pain. It's about living. It was never about dying.

I hope the heat is not keeping you up too much at night and your band is helping you escape from the madness of war. Keep your eyes searching the horizon, for it is out there you will always find your family. It is in that same place I find you when I miss you the most. Our eyes will always meet in the distant, deep horizon.

Jennifer

Here a bed, there a couch. Where before I could only find the artifacts of war in this house built by letters, now I see where a young wife watches her husband's fight unfold each night on television and waits with wrung hands for news from him, where she sleeps alone under a window open to the first winds of some coming dark night.

A flicker of light outside dances in the distance of my imagination and through the billowing linen curtains I can see small flames binding heaven and earth, the silent fire on the horizon throwing the shadow of a cross in the yard.

Yesterday by the ocean I took a step further into a soldier's heart through the deep scars of another veteran. I have yet to put myself into the year when these love letters from Vietnam were sent, because I have yet to see a road sign in Sergeant Fuller's words leading me to the landmarks of history and culture that define one of the most tumultuous years since the birth of our nation.

But now, pushing up from the dirt outside this house built by letters, is an iron post crossed by a piece of decades-old weathered pine in the shape of an arrow, with the words *offensive last January* carved in Sergeant Fuller's barely legible scrawl.

*

And I walk through the window and into 1968.

I am sitting in the family living room watching the gore of our first uncensored televised war from the last day in January. Folds of skin melted by napalm and bodies limp with lost breath and limbs dangle onto the shag carpet as we eat dinner and watch the news reports of the bloody and brutal Tet Offensive by the enemy and my dad says *Those VC are better than we've been told.* Everyone in my suburban New York neighborhood will be talking about this tomorrow because everyone watches the war on TV every night and they are starting to talk like maybe we shouldn't be there fighting these Communists, like maybe the gooks are more than we can handle or something. I can hear my brother fumbling on his guitar in our bedroom, singing his silly protest songs that he's too young to know anything about while my older sister is on the phone in the bathroom talking peace and love like she has ever since last summer. My sister is different now since San Francisco, she smokes pot in the backyard after my parents go to bed and goes to rallies and sit-ins at the university that my mom thinks are too dangerous because the crowds are getting bigger and bigger and some kids in the neighborhood are getting arrested. And all this makes me feel like I'm not part of this family anymore, like I'm not part of anything, and I want to feel part of something so as soon as I graduate this spring I will go to Vietnam, and I will find something to believe in.

Then I am leaning against a hotel balcony railing on Mulberry Street in the early evening Memphis spring twilight when I hear a single shot from across the street and in the slow frames of disbelief I see the bullet rip into the cheek of the black man standing next to me. A white man runs from the boarding house opposite the hotel as the shot man falls and I lean down and take his hand and he says to me *Ben, make sure you play "Take My Hand, Precious*

Lord" in the meeting tonight. Play it real pretty, and within an hour the Lord has taken his hand from mine.

Then I am climbing up onto the back of a flatbed truck an hour later at the corner of 17th and Broadway in Indianapolis. I look out over the mostly black crowd who may elect me President and their bodies are pushed up against each other and this sea of men and women with a broken then resurrected spirit want to hear words of hope, they want to hear that a white man like me can make things better, but I don't deliver a campaign speech. Instead I tell them that Dr. Martin Luther King Jr. has just been shot and killed and a white man has likely pulled the trigger and there are gasps and a scream in the crowd and I say what I have thought about on the car ride over here: *What we need in the United States is not division; what we need in the United States is not hatred; what we need in the United States is not violence or lawlessness, but love and wisdom, and compassion toward one another, and a feeling of justice toward those who still suffer within our country, whether they be white or whether they be black.* I tell the crowd that I know the feeling of anger raging in their hearts because I too have lost someone I love to the barrel of a white man's gun, and that loved one was my brother John F. Kennedy. I ask for peace and this city that hears my words is the only city that will see calm streets tonight.

Then I am 500 miles away within minutes of the news breaking over the radio, running down U Street in Washington, D.C. I tell the businesses they need to close except for Ms. Ali at Ben's Chili Bowl, I tell her that she needs to stay open because the cops and city officials will need a place to go and she says *yes, Stokely.* I too am angry and black and young and I have marched with Dr. King and spoken with him and already given my first Black Power speech for which I will become a leader and a lightning rod. I am only twenty-six but everyone in the street is looking at me for direction and I don't want this to get worse but I can feel a riot ready to rage out of my control. I tell the crowd following me to *go home* over and over and over and wrestle a gun away from one of the kids as he tries to rise up violence amongst his brothers. The surge overtakes my will and these activists swell into a furious mob that spreads across the street and through store windows. The point of no return has arrived, and when the violence is over more than a dozen people will be dead and over a thousand injured and six thousand arrested. Twelve hundred buildings will burn in my city alone and more than a hundred other cities will be on fire as race riots ignite and civil unrest explodes across the country. And decades will pass before this inner city I have tried to save will look anything like it did twenty minutes ago.

Then I am working in the kitchen a couple of months later at the Ambassador Hotel in Los Angeles when the man who may be President comes through the service door to greet us laborers in the belly of the hotel. I am only an immigrant busboy but Robert F. Kennedy is shaking my hand and looking me in my eyes and I feel like I belong, like I matter for the first time since coming to this country. I am still holding his hand when someone steps out from next to the ice machine and shoots this man who may be President twice in the head and he falls to the ground and I cradle his head and wrap my rosary around his hand because his fingers are not able to hold anything. He asks me *is everybody safe, okay?* and I say *come on, Senator, you can make it, Mr. Kennedy, you can make it* and he tries to talk back and all I can understand is *everything is alright, everything is okay.*

But everything is not okay.

I heard someone took a famous picture of that moment between the man who may have been President and me. They say the photograph shows what 1968 will become in this nation's memory, a remember-when of the violently changing landscape of assassinations and protests and race riots and civil unrest. I don't know about that but more than four decades later I will wear a suit and tie for the first time in my life and I will return to the grave of this man who may have been President and ask his forgiveness, because maybe if he was not holding my hand that night in the hotel kitchen, none of this would have happened at all.

*

A muted lyric whisper lingers in my throat and a tribal pulse sounds in my ears and with a primal scream that pierces like a .22 revolver blast echoing through a hotel kitchen, I return from 1968 to here, standing in this house built by letters with my fingers laced at my chest and my eyes closed. And the iconic Rolling Stones song that has brought me back in a thunder of drums and haunting wails now fills this room where Rebecca sleeps alone.

The Rolling Stones started recording "Sympathy for the Devil" in London only two days before Robert F. Kennedy was killed. When the song was first written, his brother, President John F. Kennedy, had been gunned down while riding in the backseat of a motorcade and so, in the song's broader indictment of humanity's transgressions on itself, the initial searching words in "Sympathy for the Devil" asked *who killed Kennedy*.

But just before Mick Jagger stepped to the microphone to sing the final vocal take, news of the second Kennedy assassination in Los Angeles crossed the land and ocean and crept under the studio door.

And Jagger sang *the Kennedys* instead.

"Sympathy for the Devil" would soon dominate the soundtrack running under this turbulent time of volatility and change and unrest with other songs like Creedence Clearwater Revival's "Fortunate Son" and Bob Dylan's "All Along the Watchtower," immortalized by Jimi Hendrix. And maybe the most recognizable opening two notes of the era would introduce Buffalo Spring-field's "For What It's Worth," where Stephen Stills sang that there was something happening here in the fabric of the Sunset Strip riots, something that would resonate far from Los Angeles, across the raging landscape of turmoil and conflict, but what it was wasn't exactly clear.

Those two signature notes waft in from the window on the faintest trace of smoke as Keith Richards's jagged guitar solo drifts into nothing and I follow the smoldering smell to find its source. The same words *offensive last January* that have taken me away from the window and deeper into 1968 have also framed a small box waiting under the sill for me to stand on, where I can get a better view of the shifting landscape. From atop the box I can see that the small flames on the horizon have grown closer and maybe this is where the smoke is coming from, this luminous aura that still seems to be only a sea of candles lighting the night.

And I step up and through the window and the air buoys my first footfall and then my next as I walk toward the last whispers of color, over the fire that I now know is not made of wax and thread at all and further into this soldier's heart, onto a stage in a smoke-filled cantina in Da Nang where I sing *there's something happening here* to the small crowd of soldiers and young Vietnamese women. And that something is carving a well deep in my soul and the *here* may be this bar or the deep reeds or the suburbs of east Texas. I'm not really sure.

What it is ain't exactly clear.

*

The sky high over the Pacific is cloudless tonight, punctuated by two Marine helicopters running training missions from the military base a few miles up the coast. Stella is asleep at my feet and from the couch I can see the blades rotating against the moonlight, whirling metronomes keeping time to a song I've just started writing from Sergeant Fuller to his young wife back home.

I lower my eyes and put myself behind his and he's also looking up at the night canopy of stars punctuated by two helicopters, listening to the whirling blades and hoping his Rebecca is watching the same sky. I'm here in his heart and the year may be 1968 but he's still a world away from the turbulence at home, trapped in this violent cocoon of war and all that matters is the pretty girl in the photograph he keeps by his bed, the same photograph folded into the next letter that has already fallen out of the package and onto my living room floor.

So I move my fingers along the fret board and imagine Sergeant Fuller looking out from the small window in his barracks at the sky hope painting that covers them both and singing to Rebecca under his breath so no one but her can hear. He sees a flash of light blaze across the dark canvas but this is no shooting star, this is my chariot racing across the sky as I follow the path that first song has given me, from this patchwork of stars over Da Nang to the east Texas sky blanketing a weary soldier's hope as she rests and waits a war away.

*   *   *

east texas sky

i got a bullet in my pocket
and a patch upon my sleeve
i got a feeling i can't stop it
and a feeling i can't leave

wait
you said wait
i couldn't wait

the heat here it's like a killer
your love is like a rope
i got one hand on the trigger
and one hand on the hope

wait
you said wait
i couldn't wait

so meet me tonight
in an east texas sky
there ain't nothing like
a southern girl in the summertime
in an east texas sky

i got the echoes of my brothers
they're my remember-whens
i got a young wife i made a mother
i hope i see her again

wait
she said wait
i couldn't wait

wait
you said wait
i couldn't wait

so meet me tonight
in an east texas sky
there ain't nothing like
a southern girl in the summertime
in an east texas sky

where there ain't no war
no fighting back home
no more
dying alone
what good would dying do
if i don't die for you

*   *   *

Sgt. John K. Fuller
366 AEMS DR. 43, Box 620
APO San Francisco 96337

Dear Sgt. Fuller,
This picture is on my list of family gems. You have such a look of longing and pride in your eyes because you are posing for your sweet Rebecca—her picture over your shoulder, a reminder to you of all that is good and innocent in the world. If only I could freeze that moment, that meaning, that feeling, I would suspend it for all of time.

Rebecca,

I thought that I had better take time to write you a letter while I could, so I did. I am sitting here and like always, I started thinking about you. I can't think of a better thing to do than sit around the barracks and think about my darling wife and child.

It was a little cooler today on K.P. (mess hall duty). I worked harder, but it rained and that cools things off. I feel like a cook I've been on K.P. so much. But this is the last time I will ever have to pull that stinking hose. Darling, I'm glad you are the one who washes dishes. I have washed more this week than you have in your life I bet, and when we have our own place again, please don't make me wash dishes.

Only forty-five days until I get you in my arms again. I hope the time flies by because I want you very much. Do you realize how much I love you? If every man loved his wife as much as I love you there would never be any more divorces. I feel funny inside every time I think about you, and, baby I lay awake many nights thinking about you. Just why we have to remain apart is a crime. That is enough to resent this war and U.S. policy. They took me away from you and put me here. Baby, I am sending you some more pictures. I hope you enjoy them.

I talked about you a little last night at the shop. All of the guys were telling me their tales of adventures with the whores around here and at home, and I decided to tell them what they were missing. I told them how nice it is to come in from work and find a woman like you. I like to tell the guys how pretty you are and how good a wife you are. I'm proud of you and I am happy that I found a true love that is solid as a rock. Our marriage will never crumble and fall because we are so much in love.

I know that you were afraid that I would run out on you, but as you know, even though I had the chance, I didn't even want to take it. I loved you very much then, and I thought it was about time for me to take a wife. You could not have ever forced me to marry you, Rebecca, I would have just paid child support if I had not felt the love that I did. I wanted to marry you for quite some time, but we were not adjusted to each other to marry before I went in the service. When you told me you were pregnant, I decided that we could adjust to each other later. We had to plan for a child right then, and time was of the essence.

So you see, I did love you all along, and as it turned out we have finally got our feet settled down and our heads together instead of fighting every other day. I feel like we are going to have a very sweet and full life together darling, and Jeffrey is going to have a real home. We have so many new experiences to share and a lot of loving to make up for. I know that I love you and I am going to fulfill my part in our marriage responsibilities.

Don't ever worry about my being unfaithful to you, because I feel deep inside a love that only you can satisfy. You can rest assured that if I am alone, I will be your man and not flirt with the first pretty face that comes by. I have the chance here but I will never lower myself to be untrue to you. You are my everything, baby, and I do love you.

John

For much of our lives, I remember eating dinner in various places in the house, never really organized or formal, almost unconnected. Later in my high school and college years however, we began to sit down at the table. I always loved setting the table; we all had our unspoken assigned seats. I also loved watching you eat. You seemed to enjoy the finer things in life like no one else I have ever observed. I learned to love wine and food through your selections. I always noticed that when you were done eating, you would simply get up from the table and sit on the couch, leaving your dishes on the table. We would always clear off your dishes and begin the task of cleaning.

I just want you to know that it wasn't my favorite thing to do back then, but to have more meals with you at the table now and to say thank you for all the sacrifices you made, I would gladly serve a lifetime of K.P. duty. I now understand. I also wanted to tell you that I have the china you sent Rebecca from Vietnam. We had that beautiful set in all of our homes as we were growing up and took it out of the china cabinet on special occasions. I read in one of your letters that it's a ninety-three-piece set and you paid $49.95 for it. I treasure it as part of my home now.

My honorable soldier, my father: You stand at perfect attention here and time has slipped by for thirty years to the now. You and I had a lot of very special father/ daughter moments and many conversations. We had many hurts, many lessons, and many good times. I said a lot to you over my life but sometimes the pain in my heart comes from a place that wishes I had said more and asked you more. When this letter reaches you in Da Nang and you have your life in front of you, please know that you will one day have a daughter who loves you, who honors you, who celebrates your legacy, who covets her father's characteristics as her own. You have a daughter who stands before the lens of time, at attention staring back, with a mighty salute.

I will see you in a few years.
Jennifer

I look at these pictures resting in the letter and they tell two stories, one of love and longing and one of service and respect. And I have never worn a military uniform but I have known the love of a woman, I have waited by the telephone, I have searched for headlights in the driveway. I have fought that kind of lonesome too.

Rebecca is now a clearer image to me and I still don't know her voice but I can see in this picture that she's beautiful. My eyes lose focus and her features begin to blur as I put the photograph on the nightstand in the bedroom where she sleeps. Because now I'm here, in the house built by these letters, standing next to a bed with the impression of a solitary body carved into the sheets. One half of the bed is made and one half is not and I have known this too, to reach in the night for what used to be there.

The last time I looked I could still see whispers of color on the horizon outside Rebecca's window, but now the sky has gone dark and the small points of light in the night are hidden in smoke. A hard rain has begun to knock down the fire burning in the yard, scattering the flames I once thought were only candles in the distance. I turn from the window, step around the mattress and open the bedroom door, then walk down the stairs, through the kitchen and past the set of $49.95 china that Sergeant Fuller has sent back home.

Cotton strands of silt darkness have crept in under the front door, the threatening dirt viscous thread of Jennifer's words now woven into the frayed fabric of the furniture. My fingers trace against the couch in the living room and I look down to see my palms tanned with mud and I look out the window to see the wet black soil slowly shifting and pulsing behind the house, unhinged by the chaos and turmoil of the storm. And Rebecca is nowhere to be found.

And with my eyes still blurred I pick up my guitar and imagine Rebecca fighting this tempest surrounding her marriage and family, these changes already foreshadowed by her daughter and hinted at in this letter from her husband. But she's still somewhere holding onto her own hope, as her husband holds onto his, as I still hold onto mine, which I don't have to imagine because sometimes I still look for headlights in the drive.

I think we all do.

*　　*　　*

fighter

are the lights bright where you are
do the stars there always shine
i'm still here in town
you could call me anytime

just don't call me lonesome tonight
because i don't know surrender
not without a fight

and i'm a fighter
i'm a fighter
come wrong or come right

i still breathe the mountain air
so i know I'm alive
i still go to the rodeo
i still love to watch the sunrise

i don't miss no one
no not since you been gone
i still live in our same old house
i still leave that porch light on

but you won't find me lonesome tonight
because i don't know surrender
no not without a fight

and i'm a fighter
i'm a fighter
come dark or come light

i see headlights in the drive
hear a closing car door
i see a shadow in the storm light
hear footsteps on the porch

and your voice
i hear your voice

say i drove a thousand miles tonight
because i don't know surrender
not without a fight

and i'm a fighter
you're a fighter
can i come inside

*   *   *

My frustration builds with each turned newspaper page, as the blank canvas of this new morning is torn open by the media's dark knife of all that's wrong with the world. There must be a light somewhere they choose not to see.

By the time the oatmeal is boiling over onto the stove the bad news is in the recycling bin under the sink with the front page stubbornly clinging to the plastic edge. I show the folds of newsprint temporary reprieve by pulling them out and onto the counter, where I spread the paper and wait for what's left of breakfast to cool down.

A photograph catches my eye on the second page amidst the harder news. In the foreground is a muscular, confident-looking man in profile wearing board shorts and a red shirt with the letters *RWB,* and in the background are surfboards and sand and waves. The caption says he's a soldier diagnosed with post-traumatic stress disorder who now leads surfing programs for veterans.

A scene flashes behind my eyes of the combat veteran sitting across the table from me the week before, holding his cup of tea. The still image moves and morphs and floats into his gnarled body gliding on a wave that is mending and saving his soul and helping him survive the war he still fights every day. And I wish I could somehow thank this soldier in the newspaper for the gift he's giving to his comrades, for showing veterans the restorative power of the ocean, for revealing to them what they would likely never find on their own.

Because I have seen with my own eyes this power to heal the deep wounds of war, in quiet fingers brushing the paper tag of a tea bag.

*

She says she's taken an antiwar stance and been a peace advocate her whole life, a promoter of love and acceptance who cared about every cause under the sun except veterans' issues.

Until she ran across America and found out that *she* wasn't really her.

I meet her in a strip mall south of Los Angeles. A friend has given her my books and music and this introduction and tells me that this woman has just run across the United States, raising awareness for veterans' issues and talking with soldiers from different wars as she made her way from Long Beach, California, to New York.

She's tall and athletic and blonde in a way that makes the guy behind us in line for food stare a little too long. We sit down and I tell her how I'm trying to sing from the heart of a Vietnam veteran, how I've met one older soldier whose life has been saved by surfing and how I've read an article about a younger soldier teaching veterans to surf. And I know she's interviewed a lot of veterans and this is a long shot, but the younger soldier lives south of Los Angeles and so does she and I have this feeling we're talking for a reason and does she know this soldier from the newspaper article?

She smiles and says *yeah, I know him.*

She tells me she'll get in touch with him, that he's one of the many soldiers she crossed paths with before her trek of thousands and thousands of painful, joyful, bleeding steps. She says she talked to veterans everywhere she could, from a nearby homeless shelter to the Long Beach VA Hospital, and above her in the sky I see a big blocky white building near the supermarket where my mom used to shop when I still had to ride in the back-seat. This is the Long Beach VA Hospital, where my Navy dentist grandfather was sent after he finished the work identifying American soldiers by their teeth on a warship in Pearl Harbor in the first days of World War II. And I remember asking why we never go there when I get hurt or sick and my mom saying *only the people who fight for us can go there* and not really getting what that meant.

I get it now.

I ask her why she ran across the country for a cause she didn't care about and she says that one day she turned a corner in her heart and stumbled into the hypocrisy of wanting to promote acceptance as a peace advocate while excluding veterans, all twenty-two million of them, from her scope of compassion. This is how she realized that veterans were the only group of people she *could* help and that her ignorance to their problems came from clinging to a very contrived identity that wasn't serving her any-more. And this is why she ran across the country, because she felt that she could use her own journey as a way for others to experience their own kind of empathy, commu-nity, and acceptance of others different than themselves.

She says she truly believes that we must be the change we want to see in the world, and she had to eliminate judgment within herself first if she wanted to spread that kind of love around. She tells me that she learned more about herself and the world around her from the veterans she met on the road than she can describe in words. These soldiers from her journey have become her brothers and sisters, sharing in each other's joy and pain, and that kind of connection is hard to articulate.

Many of the veterans she talked to feel like they find who they really are at war, like there's some sort of self-actualization where they discover a meaning and purpose and brotherhood they don't find here at home. Some of the younger soldiers want to go back to the battlefield again and again because this is what they're good at and this is where they belong. And this isn't about killing people or destroying buildings, this is about the only place where they can truly be present and in the moment and not in their heads, because there's no time for overthinking in the middle of combat.

And this is often the only place where they feel that the person next to them has their back.

She read a lot before her journey and learned that this kind of presence in the moment has a chemical side, releasing serotonin and dopamine and other hormones that feel good right here, right now. And when some soldiers come home and their days dawn dark, they look for that feeling anywhere they can find it, sometimes in even darker places.

I see the Vietnam veteran by the beach as a ghost sitting next to her and say *but maybe sometimes they find it somewhere better, like on a wave.* I tell her that when I'm on a wave I can think of nothing else, there's only the water and the moving through the water and no room for any kind of thought in a completely empty mind. The two settings of a battlefield and a beach couldn't be more different on the surface, but maybe somehow this is what those soldiers feel and crave in combat, this kind of satori where there is nothing but the now. Maybe they can find that here in the water too.

She says *yeah, but most of them can't find that here because they don't know where or how to look.*

I ask her what matters to them when they come home and she says *I can tell you what doesn't matter to some of them. Money.* She tells me that some of the veterans she talked to have seen so much death and destruction that money seems almost inconsequential, an invention made by a world that exists separate from their own. So sometimes jobs don't matter as much to them, either. And this makes weaving their lives back into what we consider society even harder.

She thinks what matters to these veterans is that brotherhood, belonging, and sense of service and purpose and existence that fills the empty holes that living can carve. And when they can't find the brotherhood and belonging and purpose they sometimes turn to drugs and booze and women and whatever else they can find to try to fill the holes. Or they just don't go outside because they can't separate the war there from the war here anyway.

Plates of sandwiches appear in front of us and while she talks with the server the pause in conversation gives me space to relive a memory sparked by her words *they just don't go outside.* Her eyes come back to mine and I tell her about what happened in Denver earlier that spring.

*

I was there to present some letters I'd received and perform the songs they inspired as part of a publisher's event. Later that night I played an after-show at a bar and as I was putting my guitar away a woman climbed the stairs up to the stage and said *thank you* to me.

And then without taking a breath she said that she hadn't been in a public place in almost a decade, ever since coming back from the war, but that afternoon when she heard me on the Internet in her hotel room giving the live presentation, something shifted in her. When I mentioned I was playing in town tonight she put her clothes on and as if in an impossible dream got in a taxicab and came out to this bar and waited to hear me play because she wanted to meet me.

She stopped talking and looked down nervously at her hands for a few seconds before she said *that's why I'm shaking.*

I asked her why she hadn't been in a public place in a decade and why she was in a hotel room in Denver and she said she fought for her country in Iraq but came home shattered, unable to leave the house even to get groceries, because everything she heard and saw and smelled made her feel like a bomb was going to explode or a rocket was going to fly by her head. She had read about post-traumatic stress disorder and finally found the courage to check herself into a military psychiatric hospital in Denver, which was why she was here and what she was going to do the next day.

And she said *I will take you with me.*

I wrapped my arms around her for a small giant moment and she was still shaking. She said she had to go and left the stage before I could ask her name and by the time I closed my guitar case and jumped off the stage to follow her outside, she was gone, like a ghost disappearing through a door.

I wonder out loud if this is the same military psychiatric hospital that the Vietnam combat veteran I've just spoken to by the beach had checked into four decades before. And I wonder silently if she is ok, if she can go outside now, if she ever thinks about that night in the bar in Denver.

*

The sandwiches are gone and I have to drive up the road to Long Beach to see my grandma. She's ninety-nine but not alive like she used to be, because she can't move or speak and no one else thinks she can understand anything. But I believe my grandma still lives somewhere behind those eyes so I keep talking to her.

So I get up from the table and say goodbye to this beautiful soul who has run the spine of a nation for the soldiers who fight to protect her. She tells me again that she'll try to get in touch with the man who puts veterans on surfboards to battle their demons and my fingers trace the nape of her neck as our bodies come together then fall apart.

And as I watch her fade into the concrete of the strip mall, I wonder how many veterans come back home with these holes they can't fill and these selves they can't find and these demons they can't escape that guard the prisons of their houses and minds.

Probably too many I mutter as I start my truck.

Too many.

*

I don't want to talk to a therapist he says, looking out at the shifting shades of blue through my salt-coated living room windows. *That ocean is my therapy.*

He has made the drive down here to surf, this soldier I saw in the newspaper who puts veterans on surfboards, this friend of the girl I met in the strip mall, this Marine who has served for two decades in Iraq and Afghanistan. He tells me he was just learning to surf when cowards flew airplanes into buildings in New York City and he answered their threat to our way of life with everything he had: his service, his commitment, himself. And the morning he left the ocean of home for the dust of the Middle East was his last day in the water for years.

He says he's not all that good at surfing, but he loves being in the ocean so much because instead of hot grit under his feet and in his eyes and grinding into his soul, he can breathe and move in the cocoon of cool water all around him. The air stumbling through my throat pushes out the words *kind of the opposite of Iraq and Afghanistan,* and he looks out at the ocean again and pauses and takes a slow breath in and out before saying *yeah.*

He says he has three kids now and they know not to jump on him when he's sleeping, because that kind of sudden startling movement triggers his own demons and he could react horribly, he could do something he would never want to do to his kids before he could even open his eyes.

There's a light knock at the front door before the plank wood swings open and first a running shoe appears, followed by a few stray strands of blonde hair and the rest of the woman who has run across the country for veterans. She's an artist and our talk about veterans has inspired an image she gives me of a soldier standing on a pile of skulls and staring at a house with an American flag. A few weeks ago she introduced me to this Marine and she smiles wide and comes upstairs to the living room and holds me for a moment before saying *hi* to him and tackling Stella on the carpet.

The Marine laughs and I ask him *what do you with your days,* and he tells me that he leads and supports several veterans' groups now and works two jobs while going to school at night to become a clinical psychologist. He wants to help people like himself who won't go to a therapist and before I can ask him about that irony a voice echoes from the entryway *well, come on, let's surf.*

That voice belongs to the Vietnam veteran I'd met by the beach with the battered body who told me *surfing saved my life.* I asked him a few days ago if he was in town and wanted to surf with us and he wrote back: *I have to stay for at least 8 more weeks while they try to figure out how to fix my bleeding. Somehow some shrapnel worked its way up into my upper GI, thankful that the V.A. put a filter in me years back expecting this may happen and prevented it from going to my heart.*

He's bleeding internally but still wants to surf and says that while he can't always stand up these days, he can at least ride on his belly. I'm sick with some kind of flu and almost call off the surf session until I hear a small breath whisper *this guy is bleeding inside from shrapnel older than you and still wants to surf.*

I can handle the flu.

*

And so here I am, in the water with two soldiers whose military service is four decades and a world apart, but who share this love for surfing because riding on a wave brings them joy and helps them to be here now and not in a war they can't escape. There's something else happening here, something I can't put into words yet as I watch them paddle into and out of and over waves.

All the quiet voice in my heart says is that I'm honored to be breathing the same air.

Because this is a paddle-out, the same kind of ceremonial rite that around this time last year I experienced with my friend Graham after the passing of his dad, local television personality Loren Nancarrow. We wrote a song about a letter his dad had sent me before he died from brain cancer and I remember sitting in the water late that afternoon at his memorial service, on my board in a circle with Loren's friends and family, giving thanks for the time we had with Loren and the time we have now. That song we wrote for him passed through my body as I looked around the circle, the lyric *don't cry we ain't got the time* running over and over in my head and reminding me that we must love what we have while it is still here, because our time is so fleeting and so precious. The sun went down while we were still out in the water and we waved Loren on to his next adventure, a certain peace floating under our boards and in between our bodies, a peace the ocean always brings to me when I am trapped in my own thoughts, a peace that allows nothing but this moment to exist.

And now I'm in a paddle-out with a soldier whose life was saved by surfing decades before programs existed to confront the demons he brought back from Vietnam, and a soldier who is finding his own peace again in the water while he helps lead those very programs for other soldiers.

Except in this paddle-out we aren't saying goodbye to a friend, we're saying goodbye to a war, even for just this moment as we sit on our boards and talk small-world stories and laugh and I look at the sky, the cornflower blue sky, and if I had words with enough grace I would tell you more, but all that really matters is that this is why I'm here.

And I turn to paddle for a wave and stand up on this longboard I've borrowed from the Vietnam Army veteran, who hoots *wooooooooooo* as I fly by him and I smile a small smile of gratitude for him, for the Marine paddling behind him, for the Coast Guard cutter I noticed earlier but can now barely see on the horizon over the back of the wave.

For my grandfather standing proud in his Navy uniform holding my dad, for Sergeant Fuller standing proud in his Air Force formal.

For those now and who came before them who have fought for the freedom for me to even be here at all.

*

The next morning I wake up to a note from the Vietnam veteran. And what I couldn't put into words yesterday he does for me:

Thanks Alex. Thank you for inviting me into your life, I had a GREAT time and really was stoked to meet everyone and surf with you. Wow what an amazing day very very special and will be remembered by me till I pass on. Everyone there was so special in their own life and would have wished only for more time w/each one. Let A— know that I really would love to teach her, she is a very special amazing lady, and C— is a great man and his work with vets is awesome. I don't know how he does it, I can't be around that atmosphere as it triggers too much emotion—maybe someday. And you—very amazing man and hope to get to know you better as I feel a strong attachment. Days like yesterday is why I wake up, they are one of a kind, so special and keep me wanting more. I loved every minute, nothing in the world compares to the spiritual and physical aspects of our sport, keeps me balanced and has saved my life a few times when battling depression w/PTSD. I never would have survived w/o this that we do. No words can describe/explain the total immersion in life this sport gives us. It is for sure a perfect "Heroin." Love it. I definitely want to get together with you again, I didn't get to talk to you about so many things like Idaho, your horse, etc etc etc. Hope later. —D

I will see him again.
I will see them all again.

Sgt. John K. Fuller
366 AEMS DR. 43, Box 620
APO San Francisco 96337

Dear Sgt. Fuller,
I see in your eyes in this photograph that you are weary from the journey and the night sky of life has made its mark. What do you think about so heavily? What wakes you up in the deep of the night? What do you fear the most? With the picture I found another letter you sent your wife back home, but this one seems different than the others.

Honey,
What's this about your feeling inside like I don't love you very much? I don't see how you could possibly say that, Rebecca, and it hurt me. After all I have said and done the last four months, you must not be reading my letters. I pour my heart out to you in every letter and I write more in one letter about my love than you do in three. I just don't understand. Also, you have been asking about my drinking and you don't even know how much I drink. I never drink more than a couple unless we are having a party or something. I drank more in the States than I do here. You said I would come home and turn out to be a drunk. You should know me better than that, Becky. I care a little more about you and the baby than that. I still don't believe you could read my letters and still say these things.

Another thing, you said that it sounded like I was having fun here. Well, I try to enjoy myself as much as possible here so I will be happy when I get home. If I never have fun, this place could easily change me into a cross, hard to get along with person. Remember, I am away from the two people I love with all my heart, and I miss them so much, my darling, and I miss you more than you believe. If my past letters couldn't convey my feelings, I don't know how to tell you. Baby, I fall in love with you every day all over again, and you are not even here. Can't you see how deeply in love I am? I will be expecting a letter from you as soon as possible. I don't know what else to say.

I feel like all has been in vain if you don't think I love you.

John

It wasn't all in vain. Sleep well now, rest. Your journey has been long. Love is the only thing that endures, even when we don't believe it does. Even when it appears love is far from hand. You will receive more letters, but this will be the last to Vietnam.

Jennifer

The field outside the window is black.

The hillsides are black, the once-evergreen lodgepole pines now only sticks of dead splinters hanging by lifeless roots to the loose clumps of burned dirt.

The patch of sacred earth by the barn where my horse and I were once hit hard with the dusk green all around us, in one shining beautiful early evening twilight moment of trust and redemption and love, it could have been love, is black.

The creases of my fingers are black from tracing along the fence rails that held in the containable body but uncontainable spirit of the horse, fence rails that now jut up in random fangs and pierce the air tinged with smoke and soot.

I remember looking in my rearview mirror to see my horse watching me leave for what I thought was just a short trip south to pick up the mail and pack my truck with the rest of my life. In the rearview mirror of my memory I see her following my truck out along the fence line and as I drive away I can see her reaching her head toward me over the rail. She is finally trusting me and wants to be with me and maybe I should stop and take a picture, but I don't because I think I'll be back in a week's time and will see her head reaching over this fence soon enough.

But now the fence is gone.

And the field is black.

The road bordering the field is scorched and strangely slick, almost like the black ice in winter that sends cars with out-of-state plates careening off the asphalt and into the shallow side ditches. As I turn into the driveway my tires seek traction in vain and I'll soon find that this kind of burned-asphalt black ice can't be melted away overnight or be made safe again with a change in the weather. There's no temporary solution here.

Late last night I was on the couch trying to bring another song out of these six steel strings when I got the news that the evacuation had been lifted. Sunrise this morning found me already in my truck driving the thousand miles north to the mountains, the love letters from Vietnam safe in the backseat with Stella and my guitar.

And by the time I'm able to sit on a more northern couch with the same six steel strings and look to the alpine sky and put myself into the heart of a soldier in Vietnam, Sergeant Fuller will no longer be lying in his bunk staring out the window at a canopy hope sky, he will be walking around outside this house built by letters, picking a bouquet of wildflowers from soil as black as this scorched earth.

Because soon this chariot that has blazed through the stars over Da Nang to the never-ending east Texas

deep will come to carry him home, across rivers and val-
leys and oceans and cities. And as the metal and wood of
the carriage touch down on a blackened Southern road
and Rebecca sees the headlights turn into the drive and I
crawl into his heart to sing, all I will see and hear and feel
are my own tires grabbing at this burned black ice on the
driveway, searching for a way, any way, out.

*　　*　　*

black ice

these wildflowers i bring to you
look like freedom and beauty and youth
how i wish i could tell you the truth

i pulled petals from air too heavy to breathe
where there's no time to die there's no time to grieve
how i wish i could make you believe

i tried so hard to reach you
i tried so hard to reach you

all that time you were on my mind
i was on black ice

on this highway sky i drive for you
over the pain and into the blue
how i wish i could always be true

i drive all night to reach you
i drive all night to reach you

all that time you were on my mind
all that time
all that time you were on my mind
i was on black ice
starting to slide

the way i feel tonight
i could die and be alright
if i don't make the morning light
remember the love and forgive the fight

i would drive all night to reach you
drive all night to reach you
i would drive all night to reach you
i can't reach you

but all that time you were on my mind
all that time
all that time you were on my mind
i was on black ice
starting to slide
starting to slide
all that time you were on my mind
i was on black ice starting to slide
slide
all the way home

*   *   *

I watch the moving images and look at the year date-stamped in the corner of the screen and think to myself *this can't be a coincidence.*

I've just read a news story about a decorated Vietnam veteran convicted of murdering a young sheriff's deputy during a traffic stop. His failed defense claimed that the post-traumatic stress disorder he brought back from the war fueled his psychotic rage, but he's sentenced to death and a few hours before the needle ends his life, the Bronze Star soldier says *I am proud to have been able to walk point for my comrades, and pray that the same thing does not happen to any of them.*

These grainy, halting scenes of the murder caught by a video camera mounted in the deputy's car have gained a sad notoriety. I watch a bearded man in over-sized glasses and an oversized hat and an oversized jacket jump around in the middle of a frozen Southern country road, dancing on black ice and challenging the officer to shoot him. The man charges the deputy and yells *I am a goddamn Vietnam combat veteran* and when the deputy calls for backup, the veteran goes to his truck and pushes his dog in the backseat aside to reach for something. The images are just blurry enough to not be sure what he takes from the backseat until smoke comes from his fingers and the low thunder of bullets sounds. The pain and terror and screams of the deputy are loud and high-pitched against the barrage from the assault rifle, before the words *die, fucker* are spat out by the veteran along with a final close-range shot.

He runs back to his truck and speeds away and my hands are shaking and I can't watch the video again, although I try because I see that the year date-stamped on the video is 1998.

This was the same year that the Vietnam veteran I surfed with, who walked the same war-torn soil at the same time as Sergeant Fuller, learned about post-traumatic stress disorder and took his first slow, cautious steps toward recovery and redemption.

But 1998 was a very different kind of year for Sergeant Fuller.

Maybe his demons were already walking behind him on his way to Vietnam, or maybe they found him somewhere in a field outside Da Nang. There's no way to know, since his voice went quiet before his country and his government and his town and the culture that holds them together let him speak.

Because in 1998, as another Vietnam veteran's demons take over in a shooting rampage on a cold country road in Georgia, the night sky tears open one last assault of rain on the burned earth around this house built by letters. What's left of the land begins to slide and the water begins to rise and Sergeant Fuller feels the same

long slender fingers wrap around his waist and the fire of
dead air brush the back of his neck.

And hears a final whisper in the reeds.

*

The Daily Advertiser, Lafayette, Louisiana
Wednesday September 23, 1998
Sheriff: Man Killed by Locksmith.
Victim's friends, family question official story.
Lafayette—A 53-year-old man was shot and killed early
Tuesday morning in a bizarre domestic situation that has
surviving friends and family members questioning the
events surrounding the shooting. John Keith Fuller, 53, of
101 Harvest Drive, died as a result of a shotgun wound to
the abdomen.

About 1:00 A.M., sheriff's deputies responded to a call
at the residence of Susan Goss. The woman living in the
pool house called a locksmith to change the locks on the
house because of a bad domestic situation with her boyfriend, Fuller.

According to Lt. Ken Franques, the locksmith was at
the house at 1:00 A.M. changing the locks when Fuller
drove up to the house and approached the locksmith carrying a shotgun. The locksmith struggled with Fuller and
managed to gain control of the weapon. Fuller then al-
legedly returned to his car and got a handgun. The locksmith, still in possession of the shotgun, fired at Fuller and
shot him fatally in the stomach.

- - - - -

State of Louisiana—Certificate of Death
Intra-abdominal hemorrhage with exsanguinations. Laceration of abdominal aorta, inferior vena cava, liver. Single gunshot wound to upper abdomen. *Blood/ethanol .23, positive for cocaine and THC.*

- - - - -

The Daily Advertiser, Lafayette, Louisiana
Sunday October 11, 1998
Sheriff: Fuller Shooting Justifiable Homicide
Initial report by officials notes tug-of-war for control of shotgun

Lafayette—The Lafayette Parish Sheriff's Office has concluded that the September 22 fatal shooting of John Keith Fuller by a locksmith was a justifiable homicide.

District Attorney Mike Harson said this week he has not yet had a chance to review the full sheriff's report on the incident.

However, Harson said shortly after the incident that if the case does indeed appear to him to be a justifiable homicide, there will be no prosecution.

The sheriff's office released the initial report on the incident in response to a freedom of information request from *The Daily Advertiser.*

Included in the report is a narrative of the incident leading up to the shooting and the name of the locksmith who shot Fuller.

James Chaudoin, 27, an employee of Bonnet's Key & Lock Co., responded to a call at about midnight by Susan Goss, who requested a change of locks at her 622 Bonin Road residence, according to the Sheriff's report.

Goss, 33, told investigators she was having problems with her boyfriend, Fuller, 53, and the two had been in a verbal argument earlier in the day. She complained that Fuller, a longtime employee of Schlumberger, was drunk and belligerent.

According to the report, prepared by Deputy Michael Thomas, Goss called Bonnet's 24-hour service for the re-key to prevent Fuller from entering her residence, a pool house located behind an unoccupied brick house that's for sale.

Goss told investigators she went outside to meet Chaudoin when Fuller arrived. As Chaudoin drove up the long driveway in a marked company van, Goss said she observed a second vehicle slowly following the van. It was Fuller's green Cadillac.

Chaudoin got out of his vehicle and began walking toward the pool house carrying his tools.

Goss said she observed Fuller get out of his car, carrying what appeared to be a shotgun, and began walking behind Chaudoin.

"[Goss] then shouted toward James Chaudoin to inform him of her boyfriend carrying a shotgun," Thomas wrote. "Chaudoin turned around and noticed the warning of [Goss's] statement was actually true."

Chaudoin began running toward the pool house, pushed Goss inside, "at which time both subjects barricaded themselves behind the northwest bedroom door," Thomas wrote.

Goss told investigators Fuller kicked the door open with his foot and pointed the barrel of the shotgun into the room.

"I will kill y'all!" Fuller said, according to the report.

Chaudoin grabbed the barrel of the shotgun, and the two began a tug-of-war for control of the weapon in the bedroom doorway.

The struggle escalated and led to the kitchen, where the two fell to the floor, with Chaudoin on top of Fuller.

Fuller's head struck a metal bracket located on the interior baseboard at the bottom of a cabinet, which had been open prior to the altercation, according to the report.

Chaudoin was then able to disarm Fuller. The locksmith exited the house with the shotgun. Fuller got up from the floor, where he was lying in a puddle of blood, and followed Chaudoin outside.

Chaudoin went back to his van, and Fuller walked past him back to his Cadillac. Goss told investigators she saw Fuller reach into the glove compartment, where he kept a .357-caliber Magnum.

Goss shouted at Chaudoin that Fuller had a gun, "at which time Chaudoin barricaded himself behind the front end of the car while holding the shotgun," Thomas wrote.

"[Goss said] she heard a loud blast," Thomas wrote. "She then observed John Fuller falling onto the concrete driveway."

Fuller died as a result of the gunshot wound to the abdomen.

Goss showed investigators where the altercation took place in the kitchen. They observed Fuller's eyeglasses lying on the kitchen floor in a puddle of blood near the cabinet.

Chaudoin was detained and brought to the sheriff's office for questioning. He was not charged.

*

Dear Jennifer,

I have the letters you sent to Vietnam a few months ago. I needed to let you know that your words found me, although I have always known your feelings. I am in a place now where I can feel your every heartbeat, hear your every joy and sorrow, and see the beauties of your world through the dreams you broadcast in the deep of the night. I can't really describe for you where I am, but I can tell you that you sense it all around you when your mind is still and connected to love.

I have sent you several more letters, which will arrive whenever you have questions and whenever you need me. They will find you when you are in your quietest moments, when you need to hear my voice, when you ask for them to appear.

I love you,
Dad

MESSAGE IN A BOTTLE

"Truly, it is in darkness that one finds the light,
so when we are in sorrow,
then this light is nearest of all to us."

—*Meister Eckhart*

I get off the plane in Dallas and walk through the airport to a string of taxicabs waiting outside the terminal in the late autumn evening. A torn corner of newspaper with a scribbled address exchanges hands, and while the car carries us into the center of the city, the driver tells me he's from Ethiopia and has been here working for a few years and isn't this the greatest country in the world, everyone's so free and there are jobs if you are willing to work and sometimes he thinks the people here don't understand how lucky they are. I look out the window and murmur *yes, I know* and before long the car stops and I say *thank you* and pay him and walk inside the hipster downtown restaurant rank with perfume and cologne and fancy drinks to wait for Jennifer.

My fingers brush the creased paper in my jeans pocket as I shove my hands someplace safe, away from the impeccably dressed sea of humanity circling the bar. I sense these impossibly attractive people are desperately looking for a hand to hold and mutter *aren't we all* under my breath as I pull out the yellow-lined folds and read the handwritten letter again against the low din of forced laughter and light from cell-phone screens.

> *Dear Alex,*
>
> *What I have enclosed in this envelope may be like nothing else you have been sent.*
>
> *My father died in 1998. After several years of suffering and inner exploration, I began to write him handwritten letters. The first ones were sent back into time to Vietnam where he was stationed before I was born.*
>
> *Then I began to send them to heaven. I received letters back from him in my heart, imagining what he would want to say to me if he were here.*
>
> *I feel you may have a song for me—the sender!*
>
> *With love,*
>
> *Jennifer*

And the cacophony of the bar drifts into melody and my mood dimmed by hours in an airplane and a seven-dollar beer lightens and I smile because I do have a song for her, more than one.

But I'm not here because of the letters Jennifer sent back in time to Vietnam. I'm here because of the other letters she sent to heaven, letters someone would write if they were trying to heal their own wound the size of God.

*

She sits down at the table and she is beautiful. Her long dark hair falls on her shoulders and her eyes are clear and hazel and in her I can see the pretty young mother from the photographs. In a soft Southern accent she says she remembers standing in the driveway the day after her dad died, tracing the bloodstained concrete and picking up a piece of crime tape and being so angry at what probably wasn't running through his mind in the seconds before his head hit the pavement. Her voice takes on an edge and she says *did he wish he could say one last thing to me? Did he see my face? Did he even think one little thing about me? Did he realize how badly he fucked up?*

Because as she stood there that day watching what was left of her dad dry on the concrete she finally allowed her eyes to follow the stains all the way to where this driveway led, to the pool house her dad rented for his lover, the last in a long line of mistresses and lovers before her. And this blood in the driveway became a future already eerily told in the words buried in one of the many letters to his wife, letters three decades old tucked away in a box full of tattered photographs and worn paper and torn envelopes with *Love Letters from Vietnam* etched on the top that I will carry with me on the plane back home.

If I give myself a little rope, my strong sex drive will hang me.

I saw this image of love as a rope when I put myself in her dad's soldier heart in Vietnam and sang *your love is like a rope* to her mom in my imagination. But I haven't yet read this letter with those words on Air

107

Force stationery, because the scrawled handwriting is still in the box sitting next to Jennifer at the table. All I've read are the photocopied letters Jennifer included in that package with the flower on top that she sent to me months ago. And when I do finally read that letter, after sorting through the box on my couch a few days later, I'll feel a familiar brush on the back of my neck and wonder how I could've known then what I shouldn't have known until now.

Jennifer says her dad was still just a kid trying to be a man when he got his girlfriend pregnant and married her. He held his baby boy for the first time, and a few short months later he was already in Vietnam, only twenty years old and working as a mechanic on B-52 bombers for the Air Force. And around nine months after he got back from Da Nang, another baby, this one a girl named Jennifer, was born.

Her mom told her that when her dad came back from Vietnam he started drinking more and more, but whatever he wouldn't or couldn't talk about left too deep of a hole. So when the booze only raised the cream from the dirt in his heart, he moved on to other women besides his wife, and when other women only stirred the cream he tried anything and everything to fill the hole. He finally settled on an after-work cocktail of weed, other women, and cocaine, and this is what led to a newspaper article about a justifiable homicide.

This is what left his daughter standing in a drive-way stained with his blood, following the trail of dark red streaks with her eyes up to the house he rented for his lover.

And this is what began her spiral into a deep, dark underwater cave where she couldn't breathe, at the bottom of an ocean with only the faintest of light showing the way to the surface.

*

She fidgets with the menu and says *but he wasn't an angry drunk.* After a couple of drinks he was an affable, music-playing, food-loving, gentle giant of a man and no one had ever seen the kind of meanness in him that would push him to brandish a shotgun and threaten to kill somebody. She says she's thought about reaching out to the locksmith who killed her dad, not to accuse him but to somehow draw a line between her dad and the man who doesn't seem like her dad in the newspaper headlines.

I know from reading the articles that the locksmith is younger than Jennifer and he says later the one thing that troubled him the most and robbed his sleep in the nights after the shooting was knowing that children were left behind, but no matter how much he had tried to reason with a screaming man first brandishing a shotgun and then a .357, he was given no choice but to try to save his own life.

The server is standing patiently ready to take our order and as Jennifer looks at the menu again, I wonder to myself what could bring out the John Fuller in the newspaper articles, the man who crept around with a shotgun and a .357, the man who kicked in a door and lost his glasses in a puddle of blood and screamed *I will kill y'all!*

Maybe this cocktail of women, weed, booze, and cocaine fed demons that followed him back from Vietnam, demons no one knew he harbored because he never talked about them. I remember the veteran by the beach telling me that when he came home he dealt with his pain like most men dealt with their feelings back then, keeping their nightmares close and staying silent and pretending like everything was fine, while finding refuge in any temporary escape. And I wonder now if my grandfather died so young because his heart could no longer handle the heavier drinking and smoking that gave him release from whatever burdens he wouldn't talk about after World War II.

So we will never know what kind of darkness was in John Fuller's heart that night, only that darkness was there.

*

Jennifer gives the menu back to the server and says that growing up she turned a blind eye to the fights between her parents and that she only saw her dad as a pillar of strength with a massive, charismatic, engaging, and gregarious love of life, of good food and good wine and all fun all the time. After his service in the Air Force he got a job with a big oil company in Louisiana, where he worked for the rest of his life and provided for his family.

But that day in the driveway all she could see was his bloodstained concrete love for whatever else made him feel good for a while, of not-so-good women and good cocaine, these temporary highs he chose instead of all those father-daughter adventures they talked about taking. And this betrayal hit her in the stomach again and again until the anger took her in its arms and held her for years.

She says she experienced the textbook trauma stages after her dad's death, but she felt most of them on her skin rather than in her heart. She watched a mist of shock and denial settle on her arms until the heavy smoke of grief surrounded her and sunk deep into her bones. A deep unexpressed sadness built up in her heart and forced her to retreat into the life of a recluse, a life where she could barely function enough to get through the day at work and by the time she got home, she just wanted to be alone.

She had no desire to be present in the world anymore and remembers a group of friends coming to her apartment one night and kidnapping her to get her out of her head. She can't recall everything they did that night but knows this was a turning point that led to another turning point, because they went to Starbucks for coffee and a slice of lemon bread and on the way home she had a panic attack. She couldn't breathe and rolled down the window to gasp for air, but the problem wasn't too little breath in her throat.

The problem was she could find no air there at the darkest bottom of her ocean.

But at the hospital, the doctor thought she just needed something to get past the pain and put her on antidepressants. She says the worst possible thing happened when she was taking the drugs, which was that she felt nothing. Absolutely nothing. She says *nothing bad, but nothing good, like a zombie walking around in the land of the dead.*

Not altogether suicidal, but *not* not suicidal, she was sunk into her a couch one afternoon when an episode of *Oprah* came on television with a spiritual teacher whose words ignited a small pilot light in her dark, medicated heart. That small flicker was enough to make her stop taking the pills that day and this allowed her to start feeling emotions again, which opened the door to a new, visceral anger toward her dad. She tells me that she yelled at him to *go the hell away. Stop fucking haunting me!* And she was furious with God too. *Fuck off, God and all your angels. Just fuck the fuck off.*

I ask her what she means by *haunting* and she says in those moments she couldn't hear her dad talking but she could feel him, as if he was sitting in the room with her or playing the saxophone in a song on the radio or dropping his tears so close to her they became the goose bumps on her skin. And these were all haunting reminders of how she would have to move through life without her father, reminders that if she wanted to really live she eventually would have to forgive him, which would force her to admit he was far less than perfect.

Haunted, she says, *by the truth.*

*

In between forks and glasses she tells me she knows about me from my books but asks about what's not in the books, what I look forward to (lately I'm not sure) and who I wake up next to (a Labrador) and if I have deep regrets (none so far). She says after watching that *Oprah* episode she read the spiritual teacher's book and a road of discovery opened up to another book and then another, author after author, which is how she found me and then found herself sitting in the audience in Austin at one of my shows. And when I played a few songs inspired by letters I'd received, she thought to herself *maybe I have a letter for him.*

And maybe he has a song for me.

I tell her I do have songs for her, that I've been imagining myself as her dad and putting myself in his heart
when I write and sing these songs about his love letters
from Vietnam. She lifts the black cardboard box sitting
on the seat next to her and places it gently on the table
and I can see the words *Love Letters from Vietnam* etched
on the lid. She says she found the letters in a closet at her
mom's house during a move and later, with the opening
of the lid, her transformation from an angry, bitter, hate-
filled woman to a loving daughter who wants to make a
difference in other people's lives began.

When she read the letters inside she could see how
similar she and her dad really were, sharing the same
passion and poetic nature and need for affection. She
realized he was a dreamer and she's a dreamer and she
felt like she had dug up a family diamond that shined a
bright pulsing prism of light on his heart, so she could see
him in a way she never had before.

She says *what a beautiful feeling for a daughter who lost
her father—connecting with him in a way I thought not possible again.* She felt like she'd been introduced to another
version of her dad and she could see herself maybe forgiving this version for always trying to fill that hole in his
heart with the wrong things.

My quiet voice inside says the words *the giving thing
is a forgiving thing,* words to an unwritten song that will
have to show herself later because now Jennifer is telling

me she wanted to reach through time and give him all the love he needed.

So she answered one of his letters.

And then another, and another.

Love is light and what we give is what we get. This is what the poets tell us, what the ancient prophets taught, what the self-help gurus promising easy fixes espouse.

And this is true.

*

The food arrives and in the space of putting plates on the table I think maybe when Jennifer wrote back in time to her dad, she was connecting to a lighter, more innocent version of the man he would become, and this *before* seems like a better place to begin than the *after*.

My thought is interrupted by her soft accent telling me that as she wrote to her dad, she started to see some surface light from the bottom of her ocean, but her big questions went unanswered. She was still suspended in a deep liquid purgatory between okay and not okay and still felt the aching loss cutting into her everyday life. And she wanted answers to those big questions, but he wasn't here to answer them, so she started writing to him wherever he is now and imagining in her heart what he would say back to her if he could, what advice he would give knowing what he knows now.

Because she still felt like she had jumped from solid ground to a swallowing, shifting sea the night he died, the untold heft of the shotgun shell in her hand sinking her deeper into the black. And a strong undercurrent of anger was keeping her separate from the world, unable to breathe with the viscous weight of unanswered questions crushing her chest.

She knew she had so much to give to the world if she could just swim to the surface.

And breathe.

*

She says she photocopied some of these letters and photographs in the box and sent them to me, but those were only the letters she answered. *There are so many more here I didn't respond to.* She shifts the lid until the cardboard clings to the edges of the box and takes out a photograph and pushes the tattered image between our plates and I see a soldier on a stage in uniform, singing to whoever's holding the camera and whoever's listening. I peer over the sides of the box and there are so many other photographs, so many other letters, and here's one folded with the singing photograph in a barely legible scrawl telling his wife that he's making money to send back home from singing.

He was a singer too, she says. *Like you.*

I reach down into the dusty pile of stationery and
envelopes and pictures and my eye catches the word love,
and then the word *sex*, and *body*, and then a few moments
later I see those words again on other pieces of paper. The
small quiet voice inside me warns *maybe love means sex
means filling holes means mistresses*, but the voice retreats
when my fingers find a photograph of a beautiful young
woman, maybe taken at a JC Penney portrait studio and
Jennifer says *that's my mom*.

Rebecca.

She says her mom still hasn't forgiven her dad and
threw away all her letters to him because she's still so
hurt and angry at the man he became and what he did
when he came back from Vietnam, the cheating on her,
the drinking and drugging, the fucked-up side of his dichotomy that would ultimately take him away.

And so Rebecca will remain this pretty young face
in these photographs, a mystery I will honor and respect
as a faithful woman waiting at home for her soldier to
return, a presence I must feel in the letters from her husband because the letters from her are gone.

Jennifer says the police gave her the ring that her dad
was wearing the night he died and he must have had his
hand over his chest and stomach because there was still
blood on the ring. And the blood stayed on the ring until
one Father's Day years later when she washed the gold
band in the waters of Gulf Shores and threw a message in
a bottle off the pier, the paper inside the glass sealed with

crime tape from the night he died. She says the message in the bottle was really two letters, because she wrapped a letter wishing the bottle safe passage around a letter of forgiveness she wrote to her dad.

She had hoped that sending the message in a bottle off to sea would shine bright like a beacon to light her way out of her own deep ocean. She knew that her anger was drowning both her and her dad and there was nothing left to do but forgive him, because she had tried hatred, denial, and everything else she could think of to purge the pain but nothing worked and she couldn't stay this deeply unhappy and depressed anymore. She says *there were only two ways out* and forgiveness was the only one that would keep her alive.

Sink or swim.

Her words *only two ways out* spark a flash from behind my eyes and I see myself walking out of the combat veteran's benefit on that starless night a few months ago. The cover band is playing the Tom Petty song about there being no easy way out, except this time the lyric is a whisper that cuts deeper because I've since heard the combat veteran's stories. And the stories of the woman who has run across the country for veterans, and the stories of the Marine who teaches other veterans to surf.

Stories of there being no easy way out, of not backing down.

Like this one Jennifer is telling me.

*

That message in a bottle Jennifer mentioned doesn't sound familiar. I'm gathering the air in my throat to ask if she's sent it to me when she says she now calls her dad her *beautiful fucked-up man* and we've only talked about the fucked-up side *but there is the beautiful side too.*

She pulls out photographs of her dad cooking and playing bass and trumpet and tells me that he could play anything he put his hands on, but her favorite instrument to hear him play was the piano. I murmur *that's my favorite instrument to play too* as she says their purest joy and most beautiful moments still live in her heart, where they dance around the room playing music together, her on the saxophone and him on whatever instrument is nearby.

And in my own heart I hear another melody buoying words that I hold close.

Close, because they are mine.

We dance around the room, like we used to do and then she's in my arms again / Boy I'm telling you we dance around the room and then the music ends.

And I remember.

*

"The Table" is a song about losing a best friend to cancer, a song I wrote years ago not knowing why I used the word *cancer*, not knowing that my own best friend, a Labrador named Kona, was already dying of cancer there at my feet as I wrote the lyric and melody, not knowing that song would be about a letter to her that I hadn't even written yet.

That dog went everywhere with me and inspired my first book of stories and letters and songs. I picked her up off I-80 as a puppy when I was in my early twenties and full of dreams of being a singer-songwriter. I made a bed of towels in the backseat for her to sleep on but by the time we were driving she was in the front seat next to me, stretching her neck to see over the dashboard at the long two-lane stretch of wide-open promise in front of us.

And that's where she would stay for over a decade, as I snuck her in and out of shitty clubs and hotels on the road, trying to get my songs into the world. Those quiet nights when I thought the world didn't want to listen, she did. She was my girl.

Those fourteen years went by so fast.

I wrote her a letter the day she died, which I left by her body and later tucked in a box with her ashes. The three handwritten pages thanked her for being with me for so long, through so much that I didn't know who I was before her. I told her that as I watched her succumb to bone cancer, I felt like I was watching a chapter in my own life come to a close.

About a year later I was dripping water from my wetsuit onto the kitchen floor, having just been hit by a memory in the ocean that made me rush back into the house. I'd started writing songs about letters and not really known why I felt such a strong pull to do something like that, not until that late summer afternoon when I was surfing and a dolphin raced me on a wave and the joy in that moment cleared my cluttered noisy mind to make space for what was to come. As I pulled out of the wave and the dolphin dove home I remembered that I had my own letter and my own song about it. I paddled back to the beach and ran back to the house to find those three handwritten pages in the wooden box sitting on a shelf in my living room.

I stood in the kitchen holding the letter to Kona and feeling the melody to "The Table" in the room and hearing the words in my heart, words I'd already written but not knowing they would be about this letter. Words about how my partner has been gone about a year, about how the cancer took her sudden but her spirit keeps her near. I rested the letter back on the counter and closed my eyes and saw her as that dolphin out in the water and said a silent *thank you* to her for still coming around.

That's when a knowing settled into the kitchen floor, that the letter and the song were connected, that "The Table" was written back then for a moment happening now, a song foreshadowing a future for me and my best friend, whose threadbare bed Stella still sleeps on and I trip over almost every morning.

The same familiar knowing that a song from the past is really meant for the present that crept onto the couch next to me that first time I played "Chariot."

*

The remembering lasts only a few seconds but tells me what I need to do. So I ask Jennifer what her dad would say if these beautiful pure moments of joy between them could be created again, decades later, through songs about her letters to and from his heart in heaven. Songs they could dance to in the living room of her memory.

I say *maybe music could bring you together again* and her eyes well up with tears and as she looks around the crowded restaurant trying not to cry, my eyes settle on the air above and behind her. And in the small cluster of moments when neither of us speaks I am in the house built by these letters, where she and her dad used to dance around the living room.

I step outside onto the porch and this house where the young wife sleeps under the window open to the dark coming storm, where the flames flicker on the horizon, where the wet soil creeps under the door, this house isn't in my imagination anymore. This is the house in the mountains I was packing up my truck to move to when lightning crashed nearby, still standing after the fire but almost destroyed by what will arrive next.

And I walk through this downtown Dallas restaurant, across the cracked asphalt driveway of the house in the mountains, stepping over another, but younger, veteran's blood that has been spilled there. I climb up onto the hill that threatens the foundation with a landslide after a coming storm. I see the walls and roof nestled into the wild, burned, changing mountain landscape I've just come from, where through the window I can see Jennifer washing the smoke from the walls as she writes her letters back in time to Vietnam.

But by the time she brushes the corners of her wet eyes with the cloth napkin, I think that maybe what can truly save the foundation of this house built by letters and heal the surrounding landscape are the words she writes to him in heaven.

And back to herself from his heart.

*

She's an assistant principal at a high school now. She loves working with the kids and feels like she's making a difference in their lives, and this is the light that writing letters inspired her to find after so many years drowning in the black. That message in a bottle was a beacon, as she had hoped, because writing to her dad helped her let go and forgive him and brought her out of the depths to a more beautiful life. She can breathe again.

She says her dad would be so proud of her if he could see her now, and sometimes she thinks he can. She wants to call him up every day to talk about her journey from dark to light, from cocoon to butterfly, from being lost on a rudderless ship to finding her true calling, but she can't call him.

She knows now that she can write him letters.

She says she sent me the letters because she hopes that maybe through my stories and songs other people will remember that we never know the whole story of those around us. Nobody really saw the darker sides of her dad and we don't always understand what's going on deep inside someone else, even those we love the most, let alone strangers on the street. So one thing she hopes people remember is that we all carry a burden.

I'd thought about this as I was driving home after talking with the combat veteran that day by the beach. That soldier could be next to me on the freeway or behind me at the store or across from me in an airport terminal and I'd never know the horror he lived through or the sacrifices he made or the battles he fought. I'd probably think he's just some guy in line, if I thought anything at all.

But he's carrying a burden, like we're all carrying a burden, some heavier than others. And sitting there at the table with Jennifer, this becomes compassion, first remembering that we all fight our own private battles against some sort of weight, and then reaching a hand out to ease the burden of another.

When we do, we ease our own.

Plates are cleared and when the porcelain clanging against silverware quiets she says she hopes people will also take the possibility of forgiveness with them after reading the stories and letters and hearing the songs. Because if people see that she could move toward forgiving her dad, maybe they could move toward forgiving whoever they need to forgive in their own lives, even if that whoever is themselves, and come out a better person on the other side.

I tell her that I think forgiveness seems to be for the forgiver more than the forgiven anyway, because to let go of resentments and burdens and sufferings is to also let go of the hope for a better past, which there can never be. But there can be a better present and a better future.

I've already read one of her letters to heaven filled with the words *thank you* over and over. This seems like a turning point for her and in the next small moment, as the server fills our water glasses for the last time, I wonder if this kind of compassion and forgiveness and gratitude are Jennifer's roads leading to a greater peace with what is by leaving behind the heavy burden of what was. Because if she's not overwhelmed fighting the battle between reality and unmet expectations in her past relationship with her dad, maybe she can be more in the moment and feel more gratitude for what she has here all around her now.

And she finishes my thought when she says that maybe more than anything, she hopes people will see the importance of loving what we have while it is here.

*

The check arrives and I leave my credit card with the bill in the sandwich of fake leather and she says thank you and I tell her that I feel like we're somehow connected, because we both have imagined ourselves in her dad's heart, me as I write these songs to his young wife and her as she writes her letters from his heart in heaven. I say that I'll keep imagining myself as her dad and I'll ask my friend Molly Jenson to put herself in the heart of Jennifer and we'll sing these stories to each other, to and from heaven, as songs.

Songs as bridges, connecting a daughter to what she imagines in her heart, where all that's beautiful in her father still lives, where they can dance to the faint glimmer of my guitar echoing across time and space.

I fold my napkin on the table and she says that when I send her this collection of stories and songs she'll go back to Gulf Shores, back to that pier where she washed the blood from his ring and threw the message in the bottle into the water. But this time she'll throw a new bottle with a new message, maybe a message of joy and redemption, into those waters of Gulf Shores, because this time the glass will hold my words and music.

She says *I'll put the music in the bottle somehow* and I say *so you and your dad can dance* and I get up from the table and put my arm around the small of her back and say *let's make him the first one we give this to* and then I'm gone, my heart still singing, now the last words of "The Table" repeating over and over as I walk outside the restaurant and into a cab and away into the night.

He gets up from the table and says if heaven's up to me / She's going to meet me at the old house / And slowly we'll dance around the room like we used to and she's in my arms again / I'm telling you we dance around the room and the music will never end.

And the story of the house I return to in the mountains becomes the story of a house built by letters, where Jennifer sways in slow rhythm with her dad as I play my guitar quietly in the corner of a new room I hope I can help her build.

Dad,

The year is 1970 and I am born. What are you feeling in these moments of new fatherhood? What changes have transformed you into who you are now? What are your soul lessons, the things you were meant to learn?

I am brand new to the world, experiencing a sensory explosion of touch, taste, smell and noise. I have yet to learn anything other than the sound of my parents' voices and how to focus my eyes on the wonder around me. I will have many questions in the coming years, especially in my young adulthood.

Who am I? Is there something more than this? Why do bad things happen so much? If you could sing me a lullaby that offered me the deepest of answers, a song I would remember for my whole life, what would you whisper to me in my first hours?

Jennifer

Jennifer, my sweet baby girl,

You were born good, whole, and complete. You are perfect just the way you are.

I wish I could protect you from the pain of hard lessons and difficult life experiences, but as you will learn in time, the pain more often than not turns into gifts wrapped with bows of wisdom. Revel in the beauties of living, there is so much to be in love with in this place. Yet also understand the darkness of living will set in from time to time. Never forget the light will always be present to help you find your way through. The world is a friendly place even though at times it may not appear to be.

Question everything throughout your life. Do not believe a thing to be true until you have filtered it through your soul and felt it to be true in your own heart. Many false voices will ask you to believe. Believe only what is true for you and only after careful consideration. Be curious about everything, for there are no small wonders in the world. If you see a thing unfamiliar to you, study it, learn it, and know all there is to know about it. After you have studied it and it doesn't serve you, let it go. If it feels right, allow it to be yours with strength and certainty. Curiosity and courage are among the greatest attributes you can have.

Never let the opinion of another define who you are, for what they think of you is fleeting and temporary. The only thing that truly matters is who you know yourself to be. Life can go by so very fast; slow down and be in all your moments. My daughter, there are no accidents in this world; your very birth is a miracle always intended to happen.

After living a full but short life as your father, the largest lesson I can impart upon you now is that you mustn't be too hard on yourself when you fail. Good people make bad choices all the time. Allow yourself to fail. Forgive those around you who fail. Always give your best, for if you simply do that, it is more than enough.

In these first moments of your birth, I am as happy and proud as a father can be. There is no love larger than this. As you explore this mysterious world with your developing senses, I hope what you

feel the most is the gentle heartbeat of your father
as I rock you into the journey of this life.
Dad

*   *   *

sing me a lullaby

so tell me about yourself
because i'm pretty new around here
can you sing me your answer
in a melody to keep me near

because i been so far away
down in the dark alone
looking for a little light
maybe you can take me home

sing me a lullaby
a sweet simple melody
a song for me to hold on to
a song for me to dream
sing me a lullaby

so tell me about myself
because i'm pretty new around here
is it always this hard to breathe
is there always so much to fear

sing me a lullaby
a sweet simple melody
a song for me to hold on to
a song for me to dream
sing me a lullaby
so whisper in my ear
the words i need to hear
if i decide to stay awhile
tell me why
sing me a lullaby

sing me a lullaby
a sweet simple melody
a song for me to hold on to
a song for me to dream

sing me a lullaby
a sweet simple melody
a song for me to hold on to
a song for me to dream
sing me a lullaby

*

breathe

sleep baby sleep
close your tired eyes
drift into deep
you're safe with me inside
sleep baby sleep

breathe baby breathe
what you don't see believe
in and out with me
breathe a melody
baby breathe
baby breathe
baby breathe

*　　*　　*

The house is still standing, the tightly stacked logs safe within a twenty-inch radius of protection afforded by the reaches of garden hoses in the hands of a fire crew on the wood shake roof. I leave my keys in the truck and walk through the front door, open wide for anything outside that may add fuel to the fire to be thrown inside. The kitchen is a mess of plastic chaos strewn by firefighters in a rush to beat the raging flames that have swept through this little gulch. I start carving a tunnel past the refrigerator and knock over the barbeque covered in ash and yell at Stella as she barrels through the tangle and into the back of my legs, focused in her quest to protect us from the squirrels and mice scurrying to their new homes in the cupboards.

I look through the window to the porch where the flag had been hanging for the Fourth of July, which seems like yesterday but yesterday was a long evacuation and punishing wildfire ago. When I was growing up my dad would hang that same flag outside our house every Fourth of July and Memorial Day and Veterans Day just like his dad did, but now the stars piercing the night sky framed by the wood beams tell me there's no flag there, the flag is somewhere else, her fabric probably burned to black in ashes somewhere in the yard.

I push aside the barbeque and see a flash of color to my left. At first I think maybe the smoke and fumes saturating the walls have started seeping into my consciousness, but a couple of steps later I see the flash again so I squint through a stack of lawn chairs across the room to where the flicker is coming from.

And I imagine what happened. I imagine the careful movement of a firefighter against the rush of heat and dust and wind on the front porch, I imagine the smoothing of red, white, and blue fabric, and I imagine a silent thank you to the faceless hero who has left my flag, our flag, folded military-style, there on the concrete kitchen countertop.

*

The next morning I clear away the outdoor chairs and tables and barbeque and whatever else doesn't belong in the kitchen to where it does belong until I can see the floor, which I wash with bath towels soaked in water and then again with oil soap and then again with water until the black scuff marks fade and the pine grain begins to show. I scour the walls to loosen the clinging smell of smoke, but the burn stench still lingers in the paint and furniture and if I breathe deeply my lungs rebel and my vision clouds, so Stella and I take a break to walk along the blackened road in front of the house.

There's a single streak of green lodgepole pines on the hillside opposite the house, the only sign of life left in this gulch, and I'm going over the scenarios of why those trees would still be alive when a truck goes by, slow and cautious. The white and red and yellow F-150 stops at the corner and three men get out wearing charred protective gear. They stand there and answer questions from the nonstop barrage of cars containing the tragically curious people who've been driving up and down our road to look at all the damage and quietly establish their good fortune in hushed tones that it wasn't them who lost homes and fences and ways of life.

A scene runs across my eyes of the Rockaways in New York the year before, where there are cars overturned and buildings ripped from their foundations by a bitch named Sandy and I'm there taking a few photographs. And now I'm here standing in my own destruction and never again will I be a witness to someone else's loss like this unless I'm there to help.

I approach the three firefighters and ask them about the trees and they tell me that when the DC-10 dropped fire-retardant on the houses some of the trees were also hit and stayed protected from the burn. I point to my house and ask if they were one of the crews there and they look at each other and say yes and the words don't come right away and I don't know how to thank them, because a word or handshake doesn't seem like enough.

So I leave Stella with them and run up to the house and find the last few copies of a book I've written with letters and songs about beauty rising from the ashes. I inscribe *thank you* on the inside flaps and take big strides back down to the road and give the books to these men as some small symbol of gratitude and leave them with another handshake. But that still doesn't seem like enough.

Walking back home I can see them against the cobalt sky backdrop as shadows standing on the ridgeline of the roof, defending the house with garden hoses. And this is what these men are. They are defenders, the same as the men and women who defend this country and this town and this street, defenders of a way of life, and this is why my gratitude runs so deep, this same gratitude I feel when I watch the national anthem before a football game in the confines of my living room where no one can see the thankful wet eyes.

And by the time I reach the back door and wipe the ash from Stella's paws, I'm asleep on an inflatable bed in a home office in Dallas when my host knocks on the door and says *you might want to see this* and I get to the television in time to watch the second airplane hit the World Trade Center and within minutes the streets are filled with police officers and medics and hero citizens and these first responders are also defenders, all of these civil servants are defenders deserving whatever gratitude we can muster, even through a word or a handshake or a few books.

But they can't take the dog.

*

The jutting fangs of rails and post are growing new limbs as a crew of three men pulls what's left of the old burned wood fence to make space for the new. I overhear a young, stringy kid with a shaved head and superhuman strength talking about starting a support group for guys like him as he pulls a sagging rail off a post and later, as they eat lunch sitting up against the barn, I ask him what he means by *guys like him.*

My first impression of the kid wasn't stellar because he seemed loud and badass and confident, which aren't inherently bad traits, but traits I didn't have growing up that I wished I did. Nobody would've given me any trouble if I'd been a badass.

So I wonder why a *guy like him* would need a support group.

He tells me he hasn't found much in the way of help in this small mountain town and he knows a lot of guys like him just home from tours in Iraq and Afghanistan who are having trouble wrapping their heads around what they've seen and done and felt over there. He says he's worried because at first the problems may not look that bad, maybe just drinking a little too much here and there, but the bombs and blood and bullets run deep and adjusting back to civilian life isn't that easy and he's scared of what could happen if he doesn't nip this in the bud.

And I look at him and see my grandfather and Sergeant Fuller and the Vietnam veteran by the beach and the Marine teaching soldiers to surf and my first thought is *I had no idea you were carrying that weight around.* But all I say is *thanks for your service and let me know if I can help.*

He lets me know a couple of days later when there's a knock on the door while I'm wiping down the light flakes of what used to be trees and houses that are now blanketing the shelves. He doesn't come in because his blood is dripping to the ground from his hand and I look down to see a puddle already collecting at his feet. This dark crimson on concrete is what Jennifer saw too and my eyes come back up to his when he says *I could use a Band-Aid.*

I run to the laundry room to get some clean rags he can use to put pressure on the wound to stop the bleeding, but I know that covering that gash on his hand with a Band-Aid would be like holding back the river with fishing line so I tell him *I'm taking you to the hospital right now, I just have to find my keys.*

He says no, he can't afford to go to the hospital because most of his insurance coverage through the VA has been taken away, he thinks by some Obamacare thing. I ask him how that could be possible and he says he doesn't know, but the last time he went to the VA hospital after a nail-gun misfire grazed his temple, the lady at the front desk told him that the wait to be seen by a doctor was too long. And since the passing of this Obamacare thing, nothing short of life threatening would be covered anyway, so he might as well just go home and put his head back together with SuperGlue. Which he says he did.

I stand there for a heartbeat and the quiet voice inside whispers *maybe he got misled somehow.* Maybe the lady at the front desk was having a bad day and didn't want to deal with him, so she just lied to him. But this seems so ludicrous that I don't give the quiet voice another listen and I turn from the door to find my truck keys.

It won't be long before the stories of corruption in the VA medical system will be all over the news and the Secretary of the Department will resign amidst national outrage as reports surface of veterans dying while waiting for care. It won't be long before I'm watching *60 Minutes* and see a story about the failures of a VA system where a Vietnam veteran diagnosed with a mental disorder lay in a hospital bed for eight years without anyone ever making an appointment for him to see a doctor. *Eight years* I say out loud when the story is over and I turn off the television. *Eight years.*

And it won't be long before I'll read an article that reminds me of this kid:

> *According to a letter sent Monday to President Barack Obama by the Office of Special Counsel, the VA knowingly and repeatedly ignored warnings from whistleblowers about a "troubling pattern" of negligent practices that put patients at risk. "The VA, and particularly the VA's*

Office of the Medical Inspector, has consistently used a 'harmless error' defense, where the department acknowledges problems but claims patient care is unaffected," the letter says. "This approach has prevented the VA from acknowledging the severity of systemic problems and from taking the necessary steps to provide quality care to veterans." In other words, the VA is an unresponsive, unaccountable, excuse—making mess that not only tolerates poor performance, but encourages it.

Additionally, whistleblower Pauline DeWenter told CNN this week that records of dead veterans were being changed at the Phoenix VA hospital—even now, after the VA waiting list and patient death scandal was first exposed—to hide how many veterans died while waiting for care.

But none of this has come to light yet, and right now this kid needs to go to the hospital, so I'll drive him there and put the cost on my credit card.

But in the half-minute it takes me to find my keys and come back to the entryway he's slipped away, away from the front door, away from the fence line, away from this little canyon, and into some unknown corner of the world where I hope he's alright, because besides the blood he leaves on the driveway, I never see him again.

Dad,

I am stumbling through the world. I am searching for some sense of independence. I am exploring. I am defining myself. I am learning about relationships, intimacy, and affection. I may have inherited your recipes, but I am unsure about most things. Why do you and my mom fight so much? Why do I rarely see the sweet kisses or touches of a couple? Why are you absent so much? What changes have happened within you since you have been home from Vietnam?

I often step far away from myself. Some days I feel the disconnect more than I see the beauty. Some days I cannot see God in anything and I feel like I am a pathetic broken half running faster and faster after the unattainable whole.

It seems I like to have silent feuds with God and then I feel alone and empty for every second I am away, yet stubborn in my anger. Last night I awakened from a dream in which the hidden face of God had slowly been turning so that I may see it. I am so afraid to look and the dream stops before the mystery is revealed. Who or what is God?

Jennifer

Jennifer,

You are growing more inquisitive, sensitive, and observant. . . . these qualities will serve you well in your life. The changes that you ask about that have taken place within me are something I wish I could have changed, but I was doing the best I could as I grappled with the pain of my own journey. I was absent a lot because I was absent in my own life, my own soul, fighting inner battles I cannot explain properly to you here.

I brought back a few things from Vietnam that would have been better left behind.

I had voids I was looking to fill with things other than love. Always remember those choices were never the truth of who I really am. Your mother and I did love each other very much. How well we showed that love were our lessons to embrace. Don't be afraid to let your heart streamers flow, to wrap your arms around another, to hold hands with the world whenever you can. Let your chest be filled with heart lava and let it erupt as much as you can. You can never look foolish spreading love. When you feel a void, sadness, a deep despair, seek the light of love to warm it, fill it, and heal it. You may have inherited my recipes, but you can also create your own list of ingredients. Let those ingredients be filled with color and hope, but mostly love.

And as for what God looks like, this is the most powerful of questions. Answering this question is an ongoing dance between you and your soul. It is a journey within requiring a map called Faith. The attributes I can describe as God are harmony, abundance, peace, wisdom, love, wholeness, and power.

Each one of these attributes is a chapter in a magnificent book called Life. Study each of them with your whole heart. I must also say that all of these attributes are also within you, daughter. God simply wishes to express beauty, love, and creativity through you. As God slowly shows His face through your seeking, know these are the layers of wisdom that light your journey and will result in the most profound love you could ever imagine.

Dad

*　*　*

stumble into light

last night i saw the turning
but before i saw the face
i woke in a hidden prison
so tired of this place

so tired of all the running
so far from who i am
i keep falling into questions
and the answer is you again

because i hear you softly singing
a hymn to ease the fight
could you shine a little brighter
so I can stumble into light

why is there all this fighting
where did your laughing smile go
what happened to your open heart
is there something i should know

i hear you softly singing
a hymn to ease the fight
could you shine a little brighter
so i can stumble into light

is that a candle burning

a dim light in the storm
on your face slowly turning
since the day that i was born

i hear you softly singing
a hymn to ease the fight
could you shine a little brighter
so i can stumble into light

i hear you softly singing
a hymn to ease the fight
could you shine a little brighter
so i can stumble into light
so i can stumble into light

*

the candle

maybe i wasn't around
i was nowhere at all
i know you heard me singing
i know you saw me crawl

did you see the candle
i held out in the storm
her dim light all i could handle
and all that kept me warm

yeah all that kept me warm

this aching longing fire
lit the thread in the wax
you could see my heart was breaking
you could see demons dancing in the cracks

did you see the candle
i held out in the storm
her dim light all i could handle
and all that kept me warm
yeah all that kept me warm

some things are best left behind
when the candle burned down
all i could find
was light

shine a little light down on me
shine a little love
shine a little faith
shine a little light
just a little more

*　　*　　*

My parents come to the mountains a few days later ready to work and within a week the floors and windows shine and the soot barely holds onto the darkest of corners and the smell of smoke is almost gone. Only when the wind blows through this open window does a pungent hint of fire emerge, and the night before they leave I look out the window to see dark clouds gathering behind the mountain that anchors our valley, the sunset wisps of fading red and orange curling over the black-line cumulous horizon and I ask the coming storm *where were you when we needed you?*

I'm sitting on the couch paying no attention to a crime drama rerun on television when a seven-foot high wall of wet dirt slides down behind the house and covers the streaks of red left by the young veteran and begins to push against the garage door. The landslide is silent and I don't even know the earth has moved until the increasing intensity of the lightning makes me get up from the couch to bring the horse into her small barn. As I pass the front door a white light flashes and I see what looks like thick soup rising against the windowsills and suddenly I'm on the Haunted Mansion ride at Disneyland, where strobes illuminate harmlessly horrifying scenes that aren't really there.

Another bigger flash crashes almost immediately and lights up the hillside behind the house. But the hillside is no longer there and this isn't because I'm on a ride at Disneyland, this is because the hillside is now in the driveway. And now the hillside is above the windowsills and by the time I run down the hall to rouse my sleeping parents who are supposed to go back home the next morning, the hillside is starting to come in the house under the doors and up through the heater vents.

Over two million pounds of earth has let go from the burn-scarred draw behind my house, set free by the drenching soaking saturating deluge of thunderstorms I saw coming at sunset. And the water may be able to move tons of earth but I'll soon find that no amount of rain or mud, not even a flood, will be able to wash away the veteran's blood still etched into the concrete driveway.

*

Three days have passed since the landslide. The floors once covered in soot and ash, then covered in wet soil and burned-earth debris, are clean again and the furniture and rugs drowned in mud have either been thrown out or scrubbed through to bare fabric. There are even more people now driving up the closed road wanting to see for themselves other people's problems, and twilight is falling when from the kitchen I see two Jeeps parked side by side down on the asphalt. I look closer and can't believe what I'm seeing.

There's a guy standing in the crook of his open car door and pissing in the middle of the road where my dog was almost run over earlier that afternoon by another distracted driver looking at the devastation. I explode out of the house with Stella at my heels and approach both Jeeps in time to see the man shaking the last of his urine down his pants and in the back of his Jeep I see two girls and a cooler of beer. I ask him why he's pissing in the middle of this road and don't we have enough to deal with and he looks at me and spits in the puddle of piss and pushes Stella back with his boot and says *fuck off* and gets into his Jeep and drives away, leaving behind a foot and a half of tire tread on the scorched road.

The other Jeep is still idling and I jump in front of the car and put my hands on the hood and ask that driver the same thing. He says he didn't see anything and his friend wouldn't do something like that anyway and *get out of the goddamn way* and when I come around to the driver's side I see two more girls in his backseat and another open cooler of beer. I look him in the eye and tell him to look me in the eye and the moment he does his face changes.

My eyes are almost raining and my frustration and anger are building to a head and by now night has taken hold, but I know the driver and the two girls can see my face. And I turn and run the quarter mile back up to the house before they can see what sadness and frustration may have been brought to the surface by a lost faith in strangers, with a source deeper than the puddle of piss on the street, a source deep as the scars burned and gouged into the savaged land around us.

And I don't stop running until from somewhere behind me I hear Stella whimpering as she does her best not to lose me in the dark.

*

The sun has barely risen over the ridge the next morning and I'm scraping off the last of the dried mud lodged under the kitchen cabinets with a butter knife when I hear a knock. Stella lets out a guttural warning and I open the front door to see the friend of the guy who pissed in the street the evening before, standing with a pair of work gloves in his hands. He says he can't get away from what happened yesterday, that the scene in the road replays over and over and kept him up all night and he knows it's not enough to repair the disrespect they've shown but he could work for me today, and with the confidence of a man who has stepped up in service before he says *I'll give you all I got until the sun goes down.*

And *maybe you could forgive me.*

Whatever faith in strangers I lost the day before is temporarily restored by these hands holding a pair of work gloves, but we don't work, instead I take him around the hills behind the house with Stella and show him where the land has burned and moved. We walk the whole valley looking at the destruction and there's new life starting to push through the ashes, small shoots of green here and there in the black and even a few wildflowers fighting through the debris along the side of the road.

We're almost shouting distance from the house when I find one of my dad's shoes buried in burned grass and dried mud and I remember the day after the landslide watching Stella search and search in all of her usual hiding places for the small soccer ball she carries with her everywhere, until she finally gave up. But when the first snows come she will show me that she's only let go, not given up.

As we come back to the house we cross the pasture where the two-million-pound mountain of what used to be hillside is now birthing patches of her own grass, seeds giving life wherever they land, carried here from the draw behind the house by the mud and dozers. Small shrubs of sagebrush and lupine are showing through the black field surrounding the dirt and beauty is rising from the ashes.

He gets in his truck and says he thought I was going to punch him in the face when I opened the front door. I tell him he'd be hard-pressed to find any kind of man who'd punch another man standing on his porch with work gloves ready to do something for free.

He laughs and says *forgiven?* I say *yeah, man* and we shake hands through the open window and I watch the last of my anger and resentment fade down the valley in the billowing dust left by the wheels of his truck.

Dad,

Did I get my eyes from you? I don't mean my physical eyes, or the hazel color of them, but rather what I
see through my eyes. I notice everything. The shape of
the leaves on a tree, the color of a rock at the bottom of
a stream, the way the sand forms its own castles as the
ocean touches the shore. If I did get my eyes from you,
and I am pretty sure I did, it was the best gift you ever
gave me.

I am out in nature; it is early morning and the sun
has just recently gently risen. This place I am sitting in
is so silent and peaceful it is almost loud. I can hear for
what seems to be the first time. I live in this world as it
has evolved to be: loud, transforming, fast paced, over-
stimulating—a circus of the senses. I enjoy my television,
my cell phone, my satellite radio, my computer, and I give
thanks for it all, but I know the only true way to hear my
small, still voice within is to turn it all off from time to
time. I know this voice is all around, through the rustle
of the leaves in the wind, the sway of a tiny flower, the
trickle of water, the beating of my own heart. Stillness
does speak and I am listening. The beauty of creation
speaks the loudest. I am grateful that I can see it and you
have given me the gift of these eyes.

I have always been fascinated with the lessons of the
trees. Every year, they know so perfectly when to drop all
of the old leaves and stand bare and naked in the cold of
winter. They simply let their leaves fall and blow away to

some unknown place. It must be so refreshing to release all that no longer serves them and go into a long, restorative sleep. Just as they know perfectly when to let go, they also know exactly when to bloom with all of their magnificence and color, when to rebirth and when to change. It's so beautiful that they bend and reach out to find the warmth of the sun and the comfort of each other.

Somehow, the trees know how to love unconditionally, and just be. Tell me, isn't that what we need to do the most, learn the lessons of the trees? To know when to let go, when to allow change, and when to simply bend and reach and embrace the love that is around us?

I remember sitting out in the country of Texas at our family farm. It was there you taught me how to whistle, to spit, and to speak Pig Latin, which was reserved only for the boys of the family. What I remember the most is how dark it was there when the sun went down, how the crickets roared in symphony and how the stars in the night sky twinkled with brilliance. It looked as if someone stretched a thick, black canvas across the world and poked tiny pinholes all through it. Even at a young age, I wanted to reach my hand through those holes in the Universe and touch the unknown, the brilliant light that came from the other side through the holes in the canvas.

What's on the other side of those stars? Have we lost touch with the stories of the sky?

I watch the seasons change and I long for the oppressing heat of the summer to give way to fall relief. I open *my arms to the quiet cold of winter and allow myself to lie down and let the color fall away—to lose all that no longer serves me in hope I can create something stronger. I celebrate the rebirth of spring, the warm-cool breezes and the return of color. I shed my layers and look forward to the hot sun of summer on my skin. I then begin the cycle all over again. Some days, my favorite moments are sitting in my sunroom or back patio and simply watching nature around me. I used to love to sit on the backyard swinging bench with you after dinner on weekend nights. It seemed there was always a dove sitting on the electric wires above the fence singing to us.*

You taught me how to place my hands and thumbs together just so in order to whistle back to the doves. I still hear the doves cry, and I always stop to listen when I hear their sweet yet melancholy song—in the chance I may be able to hear a little bit of you in them. Sometimes I hear you as I anticipate the changes in nature, especially the moments leading winter to spring.

I am most satisfied by the moments I can simply sit still and enjoy the here and now, knowing the color will bring itself forth in perfect timing. I watch my rosebush allow its leaves to turn red and I am grateful for this, as I know the captivating roses within that bush are only days from allowing their beauty to be seen. I celebrate the strength I see in those red leaves and I hear the whisper that says "Look at me; I made it through the hardships of winter." In many ways, I feel the leaves of my spirit are turning red. The rose will come.

But can you tell God for me that some days, it's just too much? Can you tell Him that some days, I am still very angry?

Jennifer

Jennifer,

First of all, the only way you can truly hear is to be very quiet. All the answers are there in that stillness, in the quiet.

Keep listening.

And as above so below, never forget that. The stars in the sky are the perfect reflections of our stories below and they have much to say if we stop to listen. Lie on your back in the grass on a cool spring evening with a piece of straw hanging out of your mouth and let yourself get lost in those stars. They have many things to whisper to you. It is your sky to study.

And yes, some days it does seem too much. Some days, and even at time months, the dark night of the soul settles in and what you experience is a profound absence of hope and light. God seems hidden or absent. You must remember the lesson of the butterfly when you are in this dark place. Your life journey will consist of many transformations and sometimes preceding the largest ones are the darkest of nights. Or as I like to see it, the dark night is time in the chrysalis.

The chrysalis is the mysterious place where a caterpillar miraculously turns into a butterfly.

Consider this process as you, my daughter:

You are a tiny little oval-shaped egg laid on a milkwood leaf. You grow and grow until you are ready to pop through the top of your shell and the caterpillar that is you emerges. As a caterpillar you love to chew, munch, and eat milkwood. After lots of eating, you begin to bust out of your skin. You stop eating and start spinning a silken pad all around yourself and begin the process of a complete and total body change into a chrysalis. Within this chrysalis, you liquefy and partially die. During this partial death, some of your old tissues are salvaged to form the new you.

The beautiful, winged creature emerges from the chrysalis, completely transformed.

The munching, eating, feeding, and filling ourselves up are all like stages in our spiritual growth process. We must feed ourselves with that which grows us, sustains us, and answers the great questions as we scoot along the milkwood leaf of life. This is done through studying great thinkers, spiritual texts, great philosophers, and by spending your time with open people.

Yet, the simplest way is to sit in nature and allow the undisputed laws to unfold for you, to think for yourself.

The stage in the chrysalis is a time of deep prayer, meditation, and quiet. It is the ultimate in the journey within. It allows the beautiful truth of who we are to liquefy us, melt us down, and transform us. It can be dark and confusing in that chrysalis, but on the other side of it, our beautiful wings await us. The process prepares us to take flight. Always know you can go back to that milkwood leaf and feed yourself when you are hungry, when you need to be filled up. Sometimes, you can rest and go within in that peaceful chrysalis and let divine love liquefy you. Other times when you enter, it is dark, confusing, painful, and God's light seems absent. It is during this time that God is performing His miracle. You have to trust and let go. You are finding your courage and becoming beautifully vulnerable as you prepare to take flight.

I have always seen in you the beautiful butterfly. Go on your amazing migration across the horizons. The journey, the adventure is the reason you have been given your wings.

Do you remember the times I asked you to pull the weeds in my garden and you complained about the tedious task? I know you now understand. The rose above the weeds was always there. The rose within you has always been blooming, layer after beautiful layer. The cycles of life will always be. There will always be sadness and joy. There will always be love and the absence of love. There will always be pain and healing. There will always be choice. There will always be the weeds, but above it will also be the rose.

Dad

*   *   *

crying now

stillness speaks tonight
through the million points of shining light
in this canvas texas sky
stillness speaks tonight

i want to reach right through
the tiny holes to touch some of you
i used to hear the lone dove cry
but stillness speaks tonight

is he crying now
is he crying now
if he's crying now
you know that it's beautiful

he lands silently
in the arms of this burned out tree
where my cocoon is holding me
he lands silently

is he crying now
is he crying now
if he's crying now
you know that it's beautiful

through summer thunder and autumn letting go
the rose he left here waits beneath the cold coming snow
until the spring she rises and opens to the sun
breathing in the light a new season has begun

through summer thunder and autumn letting go
the rose he left here waits beneath the cold coming snow
until the spring she rises and opens to the sun
breathing in the light a new season has begun

*

butterfly

tonight tonight tonight
these stars are doors
tonight tonight tonight

are you dark in there wrapped in blue
do you dream in color pictures
there in your cocoon

i been watching you for a while
seen that steel light shine down
on your small smile

i'm waiting here outside

tonight tonight tonight
these stars are doors
to light your flight tonight
twilight butterfly

inside in silence angels sing
let their soundless melody
lift your wing

to this southern sky
waiting here outside

tonight tonight tonight
these stars are doors
to light your flight tonight
twilight butterfly

tonight tonight tonight
don't wait no more
you and i could light the night

all i need is you
to reach through
that's all you have to do
i can see you

tonight tonight tonight
these stars are doors

tonight tonight tonight

you're a butterfly
tonight we light the night
high in the southern sky
over fields burning dry
bring the flood tonight
tonight tonight tonight
you're so beautiful tonight

*   *   *

I was a thousand miles away a few weeks ago when the sheriff began evacuating people and livestock out of the valley and just before the first flames flickered over the hillside, my neighbor loaded my horse into a trailer and took her a few miles south to a two-hundred-acre equine therapy ranch managed by some friends. Our bonds were born in horses and strengthened over the last few years through late autumn afternoon treks through steep cold-rain mountain passes and elk dinners in the triple-wide set next to the small field where my horse has been waiting out the chaos. She pushes her chest against the top fence rail and gives a low nicker when my truck door opens and I unlatch the gate, slip the leather of her halter over her muzzle, and take her home.

When I turn her loose in the field she cautiously watches the mountain of dirt for a few minutes before searching the ash for any new green life pushing through. The whole valley feels foreign now with smoke fumes still haunting the matchstick black trees and unhinged earth where there was none before and she paces the fence for a couple of days, stomping and snorting until she finds a new familiarity.

This horse with a troubled past inspired my second collection of stories and letters and songs and has taught me about trust, but more than anything she has taught me about being present in the moment. The first time I ever rode her by myself she took off like a tempest and threw me into a crumpled pile of pain in the dirt, unable to move for what seemed like a lifetime. She stood there looking at me as I lay there looking at her and in a fleeting flash I saw something beautiful in her eyes wanting to come out, some kind of spirit that had been shoved down by the ignorant hands of another human.

That spirit slowly came to the surface again by teaching her to trust in the small things and this meant I had to be with her in the moment, because she wouldn't honor distraction. If I wasn't paying attention to the present and supporting her, fear would push her into a thought of escape and she wouldn't let go of that thought until she ran and ran and ran, which is what happened that first day I ended up in the dirt.

Over time she began to honor awareness and presence and if I was with her, really with her, she'd be with me too, and before long she started carrying me through rivers and over mountain passes and would go anywhere I asked, including into my heart. Which is where she is now.

*

My neighbor brings her own horse back into the valley and in the days after the mudslide we ride alongside the burned pavement next to the namesake dried-up creek, but we turn around after about a mile because we can hear threatening claps of thunder in the distance and see dark clouds moving toward us from the west. We don't want to get caught in the kind of storm that's been passing through here lately and on the way back I notice that the dried-up creek has a trickle of water running through the small rocks lining the bottom, and within moments the trickle has become a stream as huge wet drops start to splatter onto the pavement. I get to the barn just in time to pull the saddle off my horse, put her in the field, and run up to the house before the sky starts to empty.

By the time I take off my boots, the patter of heavy rain on the roof has turned into what sounds like bullets hitting wood and I look outside to see stones of hail piling up, but this is not what drives the first nails of fear into me, this is not what I see that sends me running.

A wall of water is hurtling down the draw, banking off the slope behind the driveway where the hillside used to be and rushing down the side of the house. The violence takes my breath away because I can see the flood slamming into the fence rails, tearing them apart and uprooting the posts from the concrete and my fear rises from my stomach to my throat as I realize that this is something I can't stop.

I look down the driveway to see that the road is already under a foot of rising water and in a sucker-punch flash of panic I run to the front windows overlooking the pasture to see my horse searching for higher ground, already knee-deep in a tide she's having trouble fighting. The water is drowning the wheels of my trailer by her barn and rising so fast that I know there's no way I can hook the trailer up to my truck and get her out.

Less than a minute has passed since I heard the hail hitting the roof, but the flood has now spread across the entire valley and my whole world has moved across the film screen in my mind because I couldn't care less about myself.

I don't know how to help the horse.

*

The water is racing against my thighs down in the field as I brace myself against the horse trailer, and even if I could hook it up to my truck, I don't know if the drivetrain would run underwater or how I'd load the horse against the current and I don't have time to try something that isn't going to help, even though I don't know what will.

I see her soaked halter and lead rope draped over the fence gate, the frayed end of fabric floating against the current and I push my way through the water until my fingers can wrap around the leather. I don't know if this is a good idea to halter the horse and I don't know where we would go, maybe I could get a saddle on her and ride her out, but I can't be trapped in moment upon moment of helplessness. I must do something, anything for this horse that has only recently shown she can trust again.

I can't open the gate against the water so I jump over the fence and hold the rail as I land until I can find purchase and in that moment the horse sees me and her ears turn forward and she starts moving toward me, but I don't want her to leave the somewhat higher ground she's found. I don't want her to step in a hole or get pushed over by the hydric force and lose her footing and break something that can't be fixed, something that will make me bury her in this pasture.

But I can't stop her coming to me so I take huge eternal leaps through the flood toward her and she keeps coming, one labored step at a time and I'm almost there, I can almost touch her forelock, and now I can, I can almost touch her neck, and now I can, I can almost throw the lead rope over her, but what will we do then, where will we go, and now I can, I can almost graze her soaked knotted mane with my fingers, and now I can.

And the rain stops.

Dad,

I am becoming the rose. I am unfolding layer by layer. I am delicate and vulnerable yet bold and open with my color. I can sway in the gentle wind or be whipped around in the gust of a storm. I can allow the mist to saturate my petals or feel the heavy drops of rain shake me to my roots.

I can release my fragrance into the world and be proud of all that is uniquely me. I can allow a ladybug to cross me on her journey to the next plant. I can survive a beetle munching at my edges or a swarm of bees buzzing in my center. I can shrivel up and fall to the earth in anticipation of my new bud that needs to unfold.

Place me on a casket and I will grieve. Give me over as a rite of ceremonial passage and I will be honored for you. Add me to your vase and place me in your life for color. Give me as a token of love.

I am the rose, and I am strong.

I know you were in the room listening at your funeral when I read the Robert Frost poem to you, "Nothing Gold Can Stay." I still believe nothing gold can stay, but I do believe the memory of those golden moments can stay. The one big father/ daughter trip you and I took together to Jamaica is something I have cherished all my life and it was there, sitting at an

*open-air restaurant, that you and I shared the most glori-
ous golden sunset I have ever seen. I will always remember the way the light reflected out of your eyes and how I
wanted to reach out and touch that light.*

*The thing that thrills me the most about where you
may be now is that it is somewhere within the unknown
and you have surely touched the face of God by now. I am
so grateful with the hope that the large wounds of your
soul are now filled with a love the size of God.*

*You taught me so many things. Many of my lessons
were given to me through tough love. Other lessons were
taught with the gentle sweetness a father gives to his
daughter. Some were taught later in life after you left this
time and place. I have always been your student, in this
earthly realm and now in another time and space.*

*You taught me to give to something beyond myself
and to volunteer my time for an organization or a cause
that makes a difference in someone else's life. I learned
through your lessons that what I give will always come
back to me, including love. People need people.*

*I learned that I must allow myself to feel deeply. To sit
with myself gently and to allow myself to experience the
full spectrum of happiness, pain, or anger. I learned that
I can express my feelings or let them out in a healthy way
through the simple act of honest communication with another person or through creative outlets such as writing,
painting, or photography.*

I learned how to keep a checkbook balanced, how to manage my money, how to throw a great outdoor barbeque and light the pit perfectly.

I learned how to drive a manual-transmission car.

I learned how to parallel park.

I learned how to throw a ball correctly, how to throw a proper punch, how to jump-start a car, and how to swim.

You taught me to understand that what I think is what I am. You taught me that my thoughts can change my life.

I learned how to say no and mean it—without guilt, without fear. I learned how to say yes and give myself the chance to live life at its fullest. I learned how to cook the basics. I learned how to fish. I learned how to build a fire. I learned how to change a flat tire and check the tire pressure. I learned how to read a map and ask for directions. I learned how to work with basic tools such as a hammer, a screwdriver, and wrenches. I learned how to mow the lawn and work a weed eater.

I learned how to have authority over my own life and my own body, to never allow another to abuse me in any way and to have enough self-worth to always walk away when I am not being respected.

I learned to appreciate my natural writing and English skills, but also to work hard at math and not be limited by things meant to be dominated by boys.

I learned how to enjoy food and still be healthy. I learned to savor food, to chew every bite, to eat consciously.

I learned how to belly laugh. I learned how to cry from my soul.

I learned to appreciate nature, to see God in every-thing, and to be kind to everything that lives.

I learned to be grateful, to say thank you, and to be humbled by the largeness of life.

My dear father, I hope I said thanks enough to you throughout my life. If I did not, please hear me now.

Thank you. Thank you. Thank you.

Jennifer

Jennifer,

I long to talk to the physical you, to continue answering all of your questions. Yet, if I could return only for a few hours, I would simply want to be with you in your here and now. I would love to cook for you again—a pot of fall gumbo, the kind I made on special occasions, full of shrimp and crab claws, your favorite seafood. It would be enough to share a bottle of wine and enjoy your smile.

What I miss the most about your place and time is the feeling of a touch, the warmth of a hug, the way a heartbeat feels on my own chest. I miss the smell of coffee on a chilly morning, the way grass smells when it's freshly cut, the way my bar-beque smelled on Sunday afternoon grilling steak. I miss taking a hot shower, feeling an orange burst with juices in my mouth, the cool feeling of taking a dip in the lake on a warm summer night.

But most of all, I miss my family.

Don't take one second of your time for granted.
Every moment you have is special. Savor it all! I
know you love jazz music because it reminds you
of me. How I wish I could share the music of this
place I am in now—it is that of a thousand angelic
Moonlight Sonatas, with keys and notes and har-
monies your human ears are incapable of hearing.
My music would elevate your soul and heal every
fiber of your being if you could only hear it. I miss
you, my daughter. Besides the embrace of my love,
the music I write now is what I most wish I could
send to you.

I still speak to you in every way I can. I hold
your hand while you are sleeping; I rustle the trees
for you with a gentle wind. I fly over your head
within the flapping of a bird's wing, gazing upon
you, loving you from a distance. I sing to you with
the crickets of the night. I am the moonbeams that
find their way to your night window.

My family was my beauty, and your life and
journey is what continues to heal me. You were
right when you said love is the only thing that
endures. Be reminded of that when you forget, for
it's easy to be distracted when love seems far from
hand. I know you have forgiven me and have done
much work to heal, but know, my sweet child, I am
so deeply sorry.

Here are your dad's last bits of wisdom for now.
Be convinced that the world has more good people
in it than bad. If you truly believe this, more good
things will show up in your life. What you believe
becomes your reality. Know, from the depths of
your soul if something makes you feel bigger and

inflated with love, it is the right thing for you. If it makes you feel smaller or deflated, walk away from it. Be unalterably convinced of your faith, of your truth, despite appearances, despite fear and doubt, despite what some others may have you believe. Say you are sorry when you need to and be grateful for the rest. Your main purpose is to find that place where your love resides and make it your home. Open the doors to this place and invite the world to come in.

I know you often gaze at the pictures when your mother and I were young and newly in love. The youth of our beauty will always be a part of our story. Sometimes people let the outside beauty seemingly fade and the inside beauty gets covered with the stories of time. If we fail to open our hearts, if we live in fear, it can cause us to stand in front of a painting that was once us and long for something that can no longer be retrieved in the same way. The same place love resides, so does beauty. Age is simply a state of mind and beauty, a feeling. Although the nostalgic painting we stand in front of may be a youthful former "you" with the world at your fingertips, a new painting can be hung in the walls of your soul, one with as much if not more beauty, but with added wisdom and colors of time.

The painting of you is a self-portrait you always have access to update, tweak, freshen, or even start over again on a brand-new canvas. Paint yourself doing, being, and living the life you truly want. Live in faith every single day that you can add to the story of your painting in whatever way you choose. Literally, get out your paintbrushes and paint what you want to enter your world!

Do not cry for me or hurt for me for one more precious second. It is okay to miss me, to think of me, but know you can find me always in that place where love resides. We will be together again. Our souls will forevermore follow each other, love each other, and explore worlds together. Let this knowledge further heal you.

Now is your time, my daughter. There is no other time than now. There is no other beautiful incarnation of God the same as you, with the same incredible gifts, with the same magical purpose for being here. The place where love resides is in your heart, in the gifts you have to offer the world. You are my gift and I lovingly give you to the world.

Dad

*   *   *

maybe i'm a rose

maybe i'm a rose
starting to unfold
these layers are like petals in the wind
one day i'm quiet the next day bold
one night a diamond
next night i'm a pearl
maybe i'm a rose
but first

i'm your date at a red-dirt barbeque
where you taught me to light that pit
if i need to jump a truck
you taught me to drive stick
if i get caught in a corner i can throw a punch
but most of all i loved how much we would dance
your hand my hair a twirl
maybe i'm a rose
but first i'm your girl

maybe i'm a rose
ceremonial
saluting in the early morning light
when you grieve
if your love leaves
i'll be there when your dreams
start to unfurl
maybe i'm a rose
but first

if i need to say no i can say it strong
and saying yes don't make me wrong
i live deep
as deep as the day is long
you taught me to give when i don't have much
and i remember your touch when we would dance
your hand my hair a twirl
maybe i'm a rose

but first i'm your girl

and i remember that sunset
golden like a poem
i wanted to touch the light in your eyes
before he took you home
i hope you know
i am so grateful
that i am your rose

opening up

in the dead of the night on the side of road
you taught me to change a flat
when i am lost
you taught me to read a map
i can swing a hammer better than a boy
do you remember the joy when we would dance
your hand my hair a twirl
maybe i'm a rose
maybe i'm a rose
but first i'm your girl

*

carry me on

i miss the little things
throwing down on sundays
way out here
i miss my family
love can you hear me
way out here

i'm no saint i confess
people do more with so much less
i guess i got caught by a wrong

i seen ghosts on the river
with blessed truths to deliver
way out here

they say the truth will set you free
she sure got the best of me
i brought the rest i learned
since i been gone
for you to carry on
carry me on

now i heard some thankful things
mountain music when my girl sings
way out here
so i took a horse and a southbound train

hoping i could see you again
out here

they say the truth will set you free
she sure got the best of me
i brought the rest i learned
since I been gone
for you to carry on
carry me on

believe
have faith
live deep
believe

*   *   *

The ranch where my horse finds temporary refuge from the fire and landslide is home to a cavernous barn full of horses that give wings to hundreds of people, from autistic toddlers to septuagenarians whose brittle bones can't hold them up anymore. My friend Brienne runs these equine therapy programs and tells me she's doing a session for veterans with post-traumatic stress disorder and traumatic brain injuries and asks if I want to help.

I do and the night the veterans arrive in town I drive through the first big snowflakes of a fading autumn to hear her speak about the program at the local high school. As she climbs the steps to the stage I can see the soldiers sitting in the front row and I get lost in thought wondering if they're here because they share something special with horses, if maybe a channel of trust opens between the two that no one can really understand except for them because that's what happened to me, and I stop wondering when Brienne starts to talk.

On the surface, equine-assisted activities and therapies can look incredibly simple: people interact with horses and usually there is a smile or two. It's fun, unique, and empowering to work with horses, whether on the ground or in the saddle. However, therein lies the secret: because of the simplicity of the interaction, the relationships we forge with these animals allow for profound, breathtaking experiences. Horses are not judgmental, they live in the moment, and they are honest, powerful, graceful, and athletic. They are happy to be themselves. They are, to put it plainly, everything we wish we could be ourselves. The horse is always the equalizing factor of any interaction and for any individual on any level—be it physical, emotional, or otherwise—the horse is our mirror and gives us exactly what it gets.

When it comes to our veteran population, one could argue that the relationship between horse and human has the potential to go to an even deeper level. On the reverse side of all that our horses bring to us that is easily recognized and admired, there is a fundamental element of vulnerability, fear, and uncertainty that anyone living with post-traumatic stress disorder, or PTSD, can intimately identify with. The horse is, at the core of its being, a prey animal who has survived by staying alert, wary, hypervigilant, on the move, and somewhat mistrustful. With these traits come insecurity, anxiety, and the potential for aggression if they are threatened or perceive a threat.

Yet these very traits are the ones that can offer the most insight and the most hope: we ask these animals to go against their instinct and trust us and the vast majority of them do, especially when treated with the understanding and respect they deserve. Horses are able to do the one thing we humans have not yet mastered: they can let it go, and move forward despite their struggles, when given the tools to do so. The programs we offer at Swiftsure Ranch strive to offer our veteran population these same tools.

After she speaks a documentary plays on the screen behind her about a soldier who has found peace on a horse, but I don't see the scenes in the film, I see the Vietnam combat veteran jumping around in the middle of the rural Georgia road before unloading on a young deputy while he yells *die, fucker* and my grandfather dead of an abused heart in the driver's seat of his car and Sergeant Fuller storming through the house he rents for his lover with a shotgun screaming *I will kill y'all.* And Brienne's words are subtitles to these images where I see the soldier as a horse as a *prey animal who has survived by staying alert, wary, hypervigilant, on the move, and somewhat mistrustful. With these traits come insecurity, anxiety, and the potential for aggression if they are threatened or perceive a threat.*

When the movie ends a woman gets onstage wearing a Boise State sweatshirt and thick glasses and explains that her husband has severe PTSD and a traumatic brain injury from when his Humvee was hit by six roadside bombs in successive tours and he's supposed to be onstage now, not her, but he's standing outside the high school trying to pull himself together. She says a scene filmed from the inside of a Humvee in the documentary has triggered his PTSD, because those sightlines are his nightmares.

And she knows when he's in trouble because she also has severe PTSD from early childhood trauma, so to ease his fear they go outside and talk about how seeing the horses at the ranch tomorrow will be so wonderful and maybe he will have to take more anxiety medication later, but not until after the horses, because the horses will be medicine enough. She speaks slowly in a clear, pointed voice about how her husband is agoraphobic with debilitating anxiety and the year before, when they came here to the horses, she wasn't sure what to expect because he's scared of almost everything.

But when he saw the horses from the van he started smiling. *And he doesn't smile.* When he went into the stall of a horse named Pal, a mustang taken from the wild and sometimes fearful and anxious like her husband, he said *Hey, Pal,* without knowing this is really the horse's name and smiled. *And he doesn't smile.* When he brushed Pal and walked with him he smiled. *And he doesn't smile.* And when they're back home in the kitchen these days and he's having a dark moment sometimes he will smile and she'll say *Pal?* And he'll nod.

And he doesn't smile.

The VA man next to her onstage who has brought these soldiers here says that commitment and confidence and trust are all struggles for veterans when they come back and these horses help in beautiful yet immeasurable ways, and because the results aren't quantified by identifiable metrics, funding from the VA is hard to secure. He says the soldiers have to show commitment in the leaving of the house and town and coming to the mountains, which for some of these soldiers hasn't happened in years. They regain confidence in the brushing and handling and walking of a thousand-pound animal, when some of these soldiers have a hard time doing that for themselves. And they find trust in a safe place, as they discover the horse is a mirror, reflecting their feelings back to them without judgment or prejudice.

Then the lady in the Boise State sweatshirt takes her glasses off and wipes her eyes and says *there's something else too*, there's one thing her husband finds when he's with a horse that he doesn't find anywhere else.

Joy.

*

The silent autumn night leaves a foot of early snow clinging to the trees and blanketing the frozen ground and I follow the plow out to the highway, then south through town to the ranch. I step inside the barn converted into a cold dark office and hear the director of the ranch on the phone with the power company, trying to get electricity restored after the storm. Three men are already milling around in the half-light, two with canes and one wearing a hat embroidered with gold thread reading *USMC Semper Fi.*

Three women are lingering here in the shadows and we walk out of the office and into where the horses are and stand in a circle on the frozen ground and introduce ourselves. This is how I learn that these women are the veterans' wives and one of them says she's never been around a horse before, one is a veteran herself, and the third is the woman from last night wearing the Boise State sweatshirt.

The men don't say a lot other than they're happy to be here and I can tell they don't really know what to expect. I don't either. A tall, lanky man with a long beard and penetrating, sometimes wild eyes is propped up by an old ski pole to my left, next to the woman in the Boise State sweatshirt. She introduces herself as his wife and I make the connection that this is the man who couldn't get through the movie last night.

We break off into groups and I follow the tall man with the ski pole as he lumbers to find his favorite horse, the one named Pal. His limp is extreme and as we walk his wife tells me his equilibrium is almost completely gone from the traumatic brain injury left behind by one of the roadside bombs, and that sometimes at home he'll be standing upright and then collapse, which is why he needs the ski pole.

He finds Pal in one of the stalls, and at first I'm a little worried because I've just pledged to make sure the people and the horses stay safe and he's left his ski pole hooked on the stall-door handle. As if he knows what I'm thinking he turns around and looks me in the eye and says his first words to me.

I don't it need no more.

And he brushes Pal, talking to him in a low voice and toweling off the wet on the horse's back left behind by the melted evening snow. His eyes soften and all the time he is smiling and I have to look away, because this is so beautiful and unexpected and I don't know why I didn't expect this, I should have. This is what my horse does for me.

But this is a soldier whose wounds are torn deep through his body and spirit from the fourteen years given to his country, who won't talk or go outside, who walks slowly with an old ski pole and won't smile. And he *is* talking, he *is* outside, he *is* moving all around this stall with his cane hung outside on the rail.

And he's smiling.

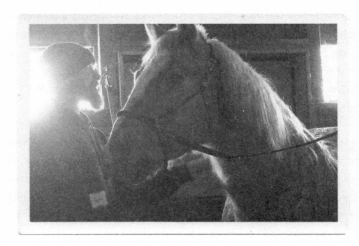

*

Small tears drop from his wife's eyes and she tugs on my jacket and says *do you see that? That's joy.* I nod and point to the cane hanging on the handle, and she says he forgets about everything except his joy when he's with this horse, and this is the most powerful lesson in being in the moment that I've ever seen, resonating deeper in me than the pronouncements of spiritual teachers preaching from stages and books that the only path to peace is through closed eyes and low chants.

Because this is about a man giving to a horse and a horse giving back to a man and this is real. This soldier is so present with this animal that what is broken mends, what is wounded heals, what is deafening quiets, and the cacophony becomes a symphony and he no longer knows what his body and mind and spirit can't do.

Life's timing is again suspicious because as he leads the horse out of the stall and toward the indoor arena, the lights come back on and the overhead heaters begin to crackle with life. I watch the veteran walk with his horse and the sudden shift from dark to light and cold to warm in the barn makes me think that there also must be an opposite to this label of post-traumatic stress disorder.

Because I've seen the black field begin to bring new life after the trauma of being burned, her strong tufts of green pushing through the ash. And people create beauty from trauma through paintings and songs and books and philanthropy. Things born in suffering, that now exist to help others.

There can be something post-traumatic other than a disorder.

I'm brought back to the barn by Brienne's voice asking the couples to pair off with their horse. At first I don't understand why the veterans' partners are here but I do now, because I see how the horses become bridges between them when the men wrap their arms around their horse and press their chests to their animal's chest and match their breathing to the horse and their wives hold the lead rope. And as I watch I feel like something sacred is starting to unfold, like I'm intruding by just being here in this moment with them.

Afterward each soldier is asked how they feel so far and the veteran in the *USMC Semper Fi* hat says he doesn't know how to explain this really but *there's an energy or something* going between him and the horse and his wife. The other wife who is also a soldier says she feels like she's more in the moment than she can remember in years because she doesn't have a choice but to be present with this big of an animal. And the lanky veteran with the beard says he can forget about all that holds him down and I smile because they are all saying the same thing and this has been my deepest, truest lesson learned from my own horse.

They aren't choking down dust in a Humvee in Fallujah or creeping through the reeds in Vietnam.

They are here.

Now.

*

After the homemade chili is scraped from the bottom of everyone's bowls we head back out to the horses for the afternoon. I lead another horse into the arena with the lanky veteran and his wife and hand the lead rope to him and we go through a series of obstacles where horse and leader have to make committed decisions to questions like *are we going in between these cones* and *are we going over this crossbar* and *are we stopping between these lines and backing up* and while these questions may seem small, they are massive in the minds of these men whose confidence has been compromised by the sudden shock of bombs exploding and mortar shells blasting in what used to be ordinary moments.

And these men must not only decide for themselves, they must decide for a thousand-pound animal that doesn't want to hurt them but needs clear direction to avoid an accident born in fear or uncertainty. This comes to pass almost tragically later in the afternoon when the lanky soldier is sitting on his favorite horse and he smiles and says he hasn't been on a horse since he was 14, *no, make that 17*, and his wife starts leading horse and rider around the arena, with a handler close by in case anything out of the ordinary happens.

Which it does. As they pass alongside an interior wall, the soldier reaches his hands above his head, stretching in an exercise of trust between him and his wife and the horse. I watch him brush the pine siding with his hand and I start to say *take your hand off the wall, take your hand off the wall*, because my horse will sometimes run from unfamiliar noises above and behind her head, noises that could be a mountain lion or something else attacking her, and this horse could be the same way. But the soldier doesn't take his hand off the wall and before I can say *take your hand off the wall* the horse's head raises up in alarm and a step later spooks to the left, leaving the ground off all four legs to sprint away from the mountain lion in the wall.

And I'm frozen in this moment because here's a soldier who spends his days in fear, debilitated by a severe panic attack from a few frames in a movie the night before. A scared man on top of a scared horse means someone will probably get hurt and I can't stop what's going to happen next.

Which is just as well, because what begins as out of the ordinary becomes extraordinary.

*

The horse is midair and I watch in my own suspended ephemeral terror as if time is standing still and across that chasm of less than a second, terror turns to disbelief as the soldier reaches down before the horse lands and gently caresses the horse's neck.

In the next half-second the soldier leans forward and says something to the horse and keeps caressing its neck and in the next half-second the horse settles down and walks forward with slow, quiet strides. And the soldier never wavers, he shows no fear or panic, because when he is with this horse he is the light to whatever darkness he carries with him through the world outside.

And they ride on.

*

The afternoon sun is dying early now as autumn hands off to winter, but a piercing light still filters through the upper windows of the barn and onto a blessed finality as each soldier stands on one side of his horse, his wife stands on the other side, and they embrace over the back of the animal by holding each other's hands. They tell each other stories, whatever they need to say, and I watch the horse become this beautiful channel of blood and bone and spirit between man and woman and I step away because I can feel the sanctity of these moments and I don't want to interfere. A handler stands in front of each horse, head bowed as if in prayer, which I find out later is true because the handlers are not listening to the conversation, they are sending thoughts of grace and gratitude to the horse for carrying this soldier and his partner in this most sacred of ways.

Afterward we're all standing together, the soldiers and handlers and wives and horses, and I'm holding Pal's lead rope next to the lanky soldier and his wife still wearing the Boise State sweatshirt. The wife who has never been around horses begins to speak but the tears and sobs take the breath meant for her words, and the wife next to me leaves us to put her arms around the crying woman.

After a few seconds she stems the tide and says that she's never seen her husband treated with such dignity and respect and caring as she has seen today. She fights another upwelling of emotion and says *all I can really say is thank you for making this one of the most beautiful days we will always remember* and my eyes well up with tears too, but as I take the horse back to its stall and wrap the halter and lead rope around the rail I wonder what happened to her husband, why he was treated so poorly when he came home. But I don't ask.

The answer finds me a few minutes later when we are milling around in the same office as this morning, but now the lights are on and the heater is cranking and there are smiles and tears and embraces all around. Her husband is drifting around a few feet to my right, wearing his hat embroidered with *USMC Semper Fi* across the back. We're told before the day begins that he has psychiatric issues and a severe depressive disorder and his wife says he hasn't ever talked about any of his experiences at war, he won't even approach the subject. This refusal to remember in words has already made me draw a line between him and Sergeant Fuller and the Vietnam combat veteran I met by the beach, and as I watched him work with a big white horse earlier I had selfishly wished they'd all been in the same war so I could draw another line.

But as he shifts from one foot to another a few steps away from me he starts talking. This soldier who before today wouldn't talk about his battles now feels safe enough to tell a war story and when I hear the words *Vietnamese girl* my body turns and opens and faces him and now I understand what his wife meant and why he would have been treated poorly here at home.

Because he's had to fight the same war that the surfer started fighting the moment he got off the plane to screams of *baby killer*, returning to his country from serving in a polarizing conflict that many soldiers didn't choose to fight, but did choose to fight with honor.

A conflict fought decades ago in a shattered land thousands of miles away, where another soldier was also stationed, writing the love letters to his young wife that now rest in a box on my kitchen counter.

Vietnam.

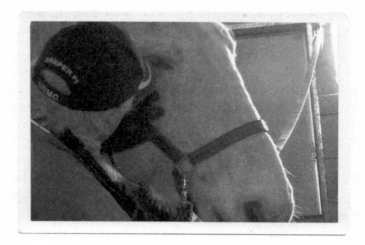

*

He says he was standing with a group of six or seven soldiers when a pretty Vietnamese girl walked over to them and smiled and worked her way into the middle of the group. She pleaded with suggestive eyes and the young men smiled back at her and a few more of them started closing the circle around her when the soldier to his right violently grabbed the girl and threw her out of the group. He kept his arms wrapped around her and pushed her *away away away* until he fell on top of her and they exploded in a geyser of flesh and bone.

Nobody saw the bomb he says, nobody knew she had anything waiting to be shrapnel under her dress, but somehow the soldier sensed something and saved his comrades. Later, when no one else really cared, at least not the privileged students or opportunistic politicians or people who hated a face instead of a war, the soldier who saved his brothers was awarded the Medal of Honor.

He stops shifting from foot to foot and says the Viet Cong were ruthless in their methods, using family members and children and any other means necessary to kill, that they were true masters of their environment and were able to melt into the jungle and disappear like fog burning away in the sun, only to reappear ready to destroy and torture and maim, and that every day he had to be ready to die. He remembers saying to himself each morning that *today is the day*, because this was the only way to fight without fear, and he accepted death with honor because this meant he would be with his brothers in arms who went before him.

And that's who he fought for, that's who they all fought for when they couldn't make sense of anything else. They fought for each other.

The only brother whose name he mentions is a black teenage kid with the last name of Brown—he can't remember the first name, but he was a singer and man, *could he throw down,* especially when the guys in the platoon would ask him to sing Smokey Robinson.

Man, could he sing.

*

After the soldiers and their wives drift into the van and drive away from the ranch and into their lives we ride along the river, the sound of rushing water and hooves crunching on snow and piercing the silence. I'm on one of the horses that have carried these soldiers through moments of trust and clarity and beauty and I'm honored and humbled he's carrying me too.

There's a house across the river up on the hill and I think I see a flag draped against a pole, but the fabric isn't red, white, and blue, the fabric is black. I peer through the trees and I think this is a POW/MIA flag with the bowed head and white print. I can't be sure because twilight has fallen and the house is on the darker side of the mountain and there's no wind to open the folds. I look in between the horse's ears at the ice gathered by the river and now feel watched by the countless soldiers not here to be carried by a horse, the soldiers who didn't come home from Vietnam and Iraq and Afghanistan and Korea and WWI and WWII and every other war.

And I know they're watching because as we make the turn off the river back toward the ranch a Smokey Robinson melody runs through me and I can hear that kid named Brown singing, his voice ringing over the decades and oceans and carving the tracks of his tears into this early winter tundra.

*

Another soundless quilt of snow covers the valley like cloth over a scar in the absolute quiet of dark and this is my sign to ease my attempts to alter nature's inevitable course by moving dirt from here to there or digging trenches to redirect next season's rainfall or clearing away burned trees. As I stare out over the still noiseless cocooned landscape I know there's nothing left here for me to heal now, nothing better healed than by the seasons.

The white buries what the fire has burned and what the landslide has carried away and the flood has carried further away and this is when Stella shows me the difference between letting go and giving up. We're a couple of miles from home on the frozen black-ice asphalt road, bound by walls of plow-pushed snow on both sides, when she suddenly bolts off to my right and disappears behind the drifts. She heads toward the creek, which has a thin layer of new ice bridging the surface and I yell at her because I don't know how frozen the creek really is. I still can't see her so I start to make my way over the drifts when she almost knocks me down coming back out to the road with a small soccer ball in her mouth.

I recognize the scuff marks and small tears around the seams and this is the same small soccer ball she treasured, the same ball the landslide had carried away, the same ball the flood had carried even further away, the small ball I now see has been buried a couple miles down the road in waist-deep snow. She drops what I thought she gave up trying to find at my feet and I take the collapsed plastic in my hand and smile and throw the ball for her over and over, all the way back home.

The land here will never be the same, but come spring the deer and elk will begin to find more new growth beckoning them to stay in green patches of still-black soil. They will beat down new trails through a moved earth and I will hear the night calls of coyotes and wolves raising new families in this changed but adaptable landscape surrounding the house.

There will be post-traumatic growth here.

But this is not yet to be. The snow signals the below-zero frigid temperatures that will close trails and leave my horse as the lone horse in this valley when my neighbors take their animals south to the warmer flatlands. A friend has a place I can keep my horse down south, so I load her into the trailer and Stella into the back of the truck and myself into the driver's seat and we travel the Great Basin Highway under a clear early afternoon sky and I think, because I think best on soundless drives through country empty of anything but country, that light sometimes must hold hands with darkness, as this bright sky will hand off to the black night hills in the marriage between mother and earth, where one is unable to exist without the other.

As the evergreens must embrace the fire, the earth must become the landslide, and the creek must accept the flood. New life will come after the storm, as happens in nature. As must happen in us.

Stella grunts in her sleep from the backseat, where she's sprawled out with her head resting on a guitar case, a small soccer ball peeking out from under one of her massive paws.

So don't give up.

*

My mom and dad come south for Christmas a day late after missing flight upon flight under the weight of winter storms. I've saved the community newspaper with a story about me turning letters into songs for a holiday benefit concert, because my mom likes to make photocopies of these kinds of articles to give to her neighbors. On her way out she takes the page with my story and leaves the rest of the newspaper spread across the counter and I push the pages over the edge to be caught by the recycling bin on the kitchen floor. As the newspaper falls I see a headline on the page where my article used to be and the breed of full-circle moment happens that makes sense looking back but rarely can be seen looking forward.

This same community newspaper I never read that gave me the story about the benefit concert for the Vietnam veteran and gave me the story about my own benefit concert has given me something else, now that my story has been lifted away into the hands of a proud mother. The headline staring up from the torn wrapping paper and card envelopes, with words visible only because my mom has taken the page covering them, reads *Veterans helping veterans is goal of "dog whisperer's" Shelter to Soldier program.*

And I'm no soldier but I have the ocean in my blood and so do the Vietnam and Iraq and Afghanistan veterans I've met here by the coast. I have horses in my blood and so do the Vietnam and Iraq and Afghanistan veterans I've met up in the mountains. But there's a third thing I have in my blood more than anything else.

Standing here in the kitchen I realize that these three things connecting me most to the blood of life and carrying me through my darker days are also carrying these soldiers through their darker days. We share the same saviors.

And I bend down and read from the recycling bin about a man who rescues dogs from kill shelters and trains them to be service dogs for veterans.

Ocean. Horse.

Dog.

*

A beat-up white car pulls in front of me on the freeway and I slam on my brakes, launching Stella into the backside of my seat. The cracked rear window is close enough that I can see the small sticker in the lower corner of the glass and the outline of a dog's paw surrounds the words *who rescued who* and I smile because again life's timing can be suspicious.

I meet him a few minutes later in front of a nondescript building just off the freeway and he tells me this is where he trains service dogs for veterans and this is also where K-9 dogs are trained for cops. When I pull into the parking lot he's leaning against the building talking to a young man seated on a bench to his left who will not move while I'm there, except for a shaking knee and a hand in constant motion through the coat of the dog that lies next to him.

The man standing says the dog's name is Charley and he found him at an animal shelter a few days before the dog was going to be killed. Charley had been moved from facility to facility and adopted then not adopted, then put on a list of dogs to be euthanized because no one wanted him. But the man saw something special in the dog and took him home and has been training Charley for fourteen months and now he's a certified psychiatric service dog, ready to be matched with a soldier who needs him.

The young man on the bench is a soldier who came back from Afghanistan a couple of years ago with severe post-traumatic stress disorder that leads to dangerous things when he has nightmares and sleepwalks. He says he doesn't know how to fix his problems but he does know that he loves dogs, and maybe Charley can wake him up before he sleepwalks and ease him out of nightmares and lick his hand when he's nervous in public to remind him he's okay.

The trainer says Charley can do all those things, but whether he will do them for this soldier remains to be seen.

Because today, here in front of me, is the first time the soldier and Charley have met.

The trainer says the dog and soldier will tell each other if they are a match and if they aren't he has other dogs waiting to be given to these veterans who go through an extensive application and approval process, because they must show they're ready to take care of an animal. This soldier and Charley take their first walk together here in the parking lot, go through some basic commands, and spend time just being with each other. Now they're both sitting calmly on the bench and the trainer says *this looks good* and they will meet again, as many times as necessary to be as sure as possible.

I ask the soldier if someone told him he needs a service dog or if he knows in his heart and he looks me in the eye for the first time and says he knows in his heart. He says he hopes a dog will be his way out of depending on his extended family, because a dog will take care of him when he can't take care of himself, like when his nightmares lead to sleepwalking and he needs to be woken up. And maybe this dog can even help him live on his own someday.

When I ask the trainer why he took this path of rescuing dogs for veterans he says that growing up he'd always understood dogs and loved working with them, so he got the required certifications and started his career in shelters and boarding facilities. He was working at a local animal hospital when someone told him about a soldier who needed help with a dog brought back from Iraq, and after the trainer agreed to work with them he saw the power of the healing bond between soldier and dog.

He says their story got turned into a book and this led to another letter from another Marine in Iraq who took in a dog with ears cut off by an Iraqi trying to foster aggression. The Marine fed the dog and sheltered him against military policy, but when the soldier had to leave in a Humvee for an assignment near the Jordanian border, his superiors demanded that he abandon the dog.

Two days later the Marine arrived at his new assignment and was working inside the Iraqi battalion headquarters when someone came in and said there was a dog outside with its ears cut off. The Marine was stunned and couldn't believe this could be true, that this dog could have followed his trail over 70 miles of frozen desert sand to be with him, and he walked outside and the waiting dog jumped into his arms.

But the Marine still couldn't keep the dog because of the strict military policy so he connected with the trainer, who helped arrange getting the dog over the Jordanian border and then on a plane to Chicago and then San Diego, where he trained the dog to be able to live in a Western environment. The dog had only ever walked on sand and didn't understand pavement and that other people besides the Marine actually existed who wouldn't try to kill him.

A month later the dog was reunited with the Marine here in San Diego. This story also got turned into a book and these were the trainer's first steps toward saving and developing service dogs for soldiers. He established his own nonprofit when the VA cut funding for psychiatric service dogs a couple of years ago, because he had seen in person how important this work was.

He says he pours everything he has into these dogs because he's an American. He was born in South Africa and grew up in Canada but got his United States citizenship four years ago and tells me he's a patriot who does this shelter to soldier work for free because this is how he can give back to those who protect this country he loves. And he tells me the staggering statistics for the number of dogs killed each year in shelters and the number of veterans who kill themselves each year and this is his way to save two lives at the same time.

Before I leave I show him a page I had read earlier that morning in the Steinbeck book of letters sent from Vietnam. Steinbeck writes that he's talking to a soldier who trains scout dogs for the military and the soldier says that the dogs can sense when something is wrong, alert the men to things they can't even see, and protect them from what they don't even know is coming and *you know, they're great for morale and give a man a lot of confidence.*

But the line the trainer repeats with a smile when he hands the book back to me is from one of the soldiers given a scout dog, who tells Steinbeck *I know him so well that I can practically read his mind.*

Maybe Steinbeck is so interested in writing about these scout dogs in Vietnam because he has a dog himself, a dog he has just taken with him on one of his last adventures around the country, a dog that inspired the title of one of his last books.

His name is Charley.

*

I hope the soldier sitting on the bench can close this chapter of nightmares and turn a new page of independence with his own Charley sprawled out next to him. Seeing his hand still in constant gentle motion along the dog's back as I pull out of the parking lot takes me back years ago to the first page of a new chapter for me, when broken dreams and a song called "The Table" about a letter to a dying dog became my first steps on this journey of songs about letters. Watching this soldier and dog disappear in my rearview mirror leaves me feeling that, like that soldier on the bench, maybe a chapter is closing for me too.

But I can't turn the page yet.

There's one last exchange of letters, anchored by a final act of forgiveness that gives a soldier the words he can no longer say to a woman who still needs to hear them. And later that afternoon, when I get home from meeting the trainer and soldier and dog and I read these last words hinted at in Jennifer's first letter back in time to her dad, I do feel a chapter closing for me as Jennifer closes her own.

Because this letter to Rebecca, this selflessly, beautifully, graciously written goodbye from the heart of a soldier to his wife, is the only letter I've received on this journey that isn't more for the sender.

Dad,

You would have been proud of Mom at your funeral. I remember watching her walk up to your casket next to your lover as she stood alone grieving over you. I watched my mother place her arms around the other woman and whisper a few healing words. That is strength. That is forgiveness.

Jennifer

Jennifer,

Please tell your mother I was there watching and there was never a moment I learned more from her beauty. When we give, our hands are never empty. Love will create abundance in every aspect of your life and no one can ever stop you from loving.

Forgiveness is a gift you give yourself.

Here is that last big letter you were asking for.

Love,

Dad

My Dear Wife, Rebecca,

On April 5, 1966, I was given the most precious of life's gifts, your hand in marriage. Of all the memories that have stayed rooted within my spirit, the one that shines the brightest is how beautiful you looked in that flowing, white wedding dress and how strong and proud I felt in my U.S. Air Force formal. No divorce paper could ever nullify how much I loved you, even when the times were bad and we were both doing the best we could with what we knew.

Regardless of anything you may think or feel about me, you are the one and only true love of my lifetime. If I were to write you only three words and have the sacred meaning of those words find your heart truly and deeply, I would write "I love you" across the Southern skies and that would be enough.

If I could go back to one place and time in my lifetime, it would be September 28 of 1968 in Hawaii. It was in Hawaii we met for my military R&R and it was also the honeymoon we never got to take. I longed and ached for you during those many months away from you. There was no sweeter time than when my eyes locked with yours on that beautiful island.

That was my heaven on earth.

With you and through you, I went from boy, to father, to soldier, to husband, to man. In that evolution, I was an imperfect man much of the time. I know you carry the scars of burden in your heart from my imperfections. There is much to say about forgiveness and letting go. If I could send a few simple messages from where I am to where you are, it would be that life on earth is about loving. It's about the adventures of being alive, of giving back more than you take and evolving as a spirit through the many lessons life provides.

The lesson of forgiveness is one of the hardest to learn, but it is the one lesson that gives us the greatest freedom.

Forgiveness is never about making whatever transgression someone has committed against you okay.

Forgiveness is for yourself and being able to give yourself the gift of letting go of pain, resentment, and anger. This freedom opens the door to love and happiness. This freedom heals you.

Rebecca, please forgive me and allow the release that comes with this to free your beautiful heart. Also know that in the place I am in now, forgiving myself was my biggest challenge. I have accounted for my mistakes and relived the consequences a thousand times over. The freedom I can now experience is beyond anything I can describe in human terms. I want you to have that same freedom too.

I ask you to hold on to the pieces of me that continue to serve you. At the top of that list should be my deep and abounding love for you that will go on through the millennia. No one or no thing can ever diminish my love for you; it is among the strongest forces in the Universe. Hold on to our two precious children and their children, for they are the ultimate product of our love and my most profound pride.

Let go of the rest of it. Let go of me, of the painful memories, of the dark thoughts buried deep in your consciousness.

Thank you for all the love you have given me, for the sacrifices, for the honor of allowing me to call you wife. You spent the morning of your life with me, through its gorgeous sunrises and its tumultuous thunderstorms. I

*am grateful for every moment of your love. Now, it is the
evening of your life and there is so much that awaits you.
There is much adventure, many starlit nights, full moons,
and new love that calls for you. Be free.*

The twilight of your life is before you.

Always,

John

*

I rest the guitar on the couch and let a slow breath escape into the living room, now darkening with winter twilight. I close my eyes and I'm in a familiar hallway with a flickering bulb sparking and hissing above my head. I see a hole in the ceiling at the end of the hallway with soft light spilling down and I walk toward the glow, past the room where the young wife sleeps with the window open to the coming storms and the couch where she watches the war on television. My fingers trace the walls hung with letters on Air Force stationery and wartorn photographs, and before I ascend the stairs falling from the hole in the ceiling my hand touches the picture frame around my grandfather holding my dad. I look at the uniform, the smile, the shoes of the little boy who would become my father, and I bow my head.

One slow step at a time with my hand on the bannister I rise and stop at the top and turn slowly toward the light and they are there. A proud soldier in his formal with a patch on his sleeve and his beautiful young wife dressed in white chiffon stand holding hands, facing each other on a shining new wood floor. My weathered guitar leans against a chair in the far corner and I move toward the wood and wire and the soldier and wife don't move and I take the guitar in my hands and they don't move and I sit down on the chair and they don't move and I begin to play and they move, in slow sweeping arcs they dance.

I hear a rustle in the shadows by the stairs, and a dark figure approaches the wife and reaches out and my quiet voice silently pleads *please don't be the long slender fingers of my dreams in the reeds, please don't be please don't be.*

But there are no long slender fingers, only a small delicate hand coming to rest softly on the shoulder of the wife.

And the wife turns to embrace her daughter and steps away from her husband and back into the shadows and the soldier holds his daughter and twirls her hair and they dance around the room like they used to do and she's in his arms again.

*   *   *

twilight

love look at you now
i have never been so proud
as tonight
my angel in white

love look at you now
southern boy in luck somehow
when we met
and a man when you left

and if i made you cry
your tears are mine
tonight
in the twilight

remember 68
love i couldn't wait
to see you then
and touch you again

so now take my hand
in yours as we dance
across the floor
could you love me more

and if i made you cry
your tears are mine
tonight
in the twilight
and i shine when you shine
your eyes are mine
tonight
in the twilight

because the living thing
is a forgiving thing
let go of everything

hear the guitar sing

in the twilight
we dance around the room
like we used to do
in the twilight

*   *   *

CODA *(music)*

concluding passage—It. L. cauda: tail

*"Someday after mastering the winds, the waves, the tides
and gravity, we shall harness for God the energies of love,
and then, for a second time in the history of the world,
man will have discovered fire."*

—*Pierre Teilhard de Chardin*

Stella comes into the kitchen from the bedroom, where earlier that morning the walls echoed her loud bark of concern tinged with aggression for whatever demons I dreamed in the reeds, whatever lurks beneath my consciousness at night as I've put myself further behind a soldier's eyes during the day. Her already strong protective streak must extend to the netherworld, and when coupled with her fierce oceanic adventures at dawn there's not a lot left in the tank, because she stretches and yawns and eyes the ball lodged under the dishwasher before thinking better of any kind of afternoon activity, other than flopping her hundred pounds down thunderously at my feet with a low groan that says she too is getting older.

I trace her spine gently with my foot and offer a silent prayer that the day is still far away when I'll miss her like I still sometimes miss her sister, to whom I once wrote a letter and for whom I still sing a song written in my first blind steps on this journey.

The box with *Love Letters from Vietnam* etched on top is sitting on the counter, the letters and photographs and newspaper articles scattered around tiredly as if their work and travel over oceans and continents and decades is done. These scrawled words on creased paper from a soldier to his girl, so simply written more for the sender, are a serviceman's only link to his beloved and his world back home. And the frayed edges of Kodak paper remind me that in this time of immediate contact and images on screens of artificial glow, these handwritten words and moments burned dark and light are as sacred as these letters written in a circle between a daughter and the heart of the father still beating in her chest.

Standing there shuffling the memories on the counter, I remember what I sometimes forget. Forgiveness. Compassion. Gratitude. Three roads leading to being here now, where we can give the next moment a chance to exist without prejudice, so we can love what's here, while it's still here: each other, ourselves, our freedom.

Jennifer and I talked about those roads at that restaurant in Dallas, and as I begin to stack the letters back into the box I can still hear her mentioning a message in a bottle and talking about the beauty and meaning and power in letting the glass float out to sea. I can still feel myself almost ask her if she had a copy of the message somewhere that she could send me, before the conversation took a turn somewhere else.

But I've had the message in a bottle here with me the whole time.

*

Hi Alex,

I talked to Wendy today on the phone and I am so happy she confirmed you will be using my letter(s) in your next book. I completely let go of any attachments to the final product. You will with no doubt make something beautiful and healing.

I did want to include one last thing: the original letter I wrote to my dad.

On a Father's Day when I was just starting this journey, I put two handwritten letters in a sealed bottle before we drove to the beach in Gulf Shores, which was my dad's favorite place. Standing on the pier I felt a moment of joyful release and surrender as I threw the bottle into the ocean and watched it drift away, holding my messages of forgiveness and hope for safe passage to whatever or whoever the bottle was supposed to find.

The bottle found you.

With gratitude,

Jennifer Fuller

My Dearest Ocean's Bottle:

Today is Father's Day, and I have decided to once and for all let this go and make a commitment to myself to heal on all levels. I place this message in you with a few relics and the yellow piece of crime tape I have kept in my possession for all these years. The day after it happened, I had to stand in the very place my father had fallen in blood, to confirm for myself that he was gone. The area was still surrounded with yellow crime-scene tape, and I bent down to shove a piece in my pocket, thus beginning the dark-to-light journey.

The Gulf Coast between Alabama and Florida has always been a special spot for our family. We have come here year after year, and after my father's death, I have kept this place alive for us by returning with my mother each summer. These waves, this shoreline, hold the memory of my father, and his sound will always resonate in the waves.

I have a lot to feel sad about or angry about when I think of the events surrounding his death. I cannot dwell on those things for one second longer. I can no longer carry these wounds like a flag hoisted from my heart announcing the reality of a disconnected, ungrounded, angry soul.

When I look at pictures of him now, the handsome golfer, delightful chef, blues-lovin' soul man, I can see an ache in his eyes for love, for the feeling of freedom from earthly entanglements, and I see the sparkle of the healing vibrations of a bass guitar strummed from within his heart.

For the past several years, all he has been to me is a sadly laminated obituary, a box full of newspaper clippings and relics of a ghost I have damned and cursed.

Today, and upon tossing you, my healing bottle, into the sea . . . I wish for him to be a released, beautiful spirit, rocking in the lap of God, the beautiful man I knew him to be. Though imperfect here as my father, he is now perfect and completely set free in the healing breath of heaven, surrounded by angels and saints and great mystics.

I have stored his golden ring in a box in my closet, still stained with a drop of blood from that dark night. This ring will be washed in the salty waves of the Gulf of Mexico and given to my brother to wear proudly, for he is the only logical holder of a ring that represents strength, creativity, and the lessons learned from a chapter of life called Our Dad.

I include in you this letter to him.
Dear Dad,

May you now become in my heart what you have always been: giver of my life, teacher, athlete, musician, chef, life of the party, healer. I know now that your energy is not gone; it just lives on in a different form, one that I cannot see or hear, but one that I can sense if I open my heart.

Your memory will always stay golden until the day I join you in the lap of God. I will cherish all the gifts you have left me and all the lessons written and planted in the depths of my heart.

And when things get difficult for me as they sometimes do, I will remember your boyish grin, the comfort of your crackling knees as you walk down the hall, and the twirl of my hair during a daughter/father dance on our living room floor. May all Father's Days from now on be a day of celebration and thankfulness, not a day of sadness and loss.

With a glass of wine, a wonderful meal, the sound of a saxophone, the tune of a dove, the smell of the ocean, the back porch at dusk, a pot of gumbo, the fragrance of a rose. . . .

Happy Father's Day.

I love you,

Jennifer

And now, dear bottle, I humbly cast you to the ocean and bid you on a journey only a thing released from my soul could wander to. May your glass peacefully perspire in the sun's warming arms, may you twinkle like a blanket of faraway stars. May you float waywardly, allowing heaven's compass to be your guide. You contain tears and suffering, memories of a forever united and scarred family, but mostly you contain love and healing energy, only possible because I allow it to be in this very moment.

With the release of my hand, I toss you to the Universe, and I ask the ebb and flow to deliver you to my father.

   To what you may find,
   Jennifer

*

And so I give you the story of how this message in a bottle found me, carried by winds of service, waves of gratitude, tides of compassion, and the final gravity of forgiveness.

Whether I've harnessed love and discovered fire with these words remains to be seen.

Because, you see, the bottle has now found you.

RESOURCES

for veterans and their loved ones

www.sheltertosoldier.org

www.teamrwb.org

www.therapydogcertification.com/
6-organizations-that-provide-therapy-dogs-for-veterans

www.veteranscrisisline.net/gethelp/resourcelocator.aspx

www.nami.org

www.jobcenter.usa.gov/resources-for-veterans

www.vetsresource.org

www.mentalhealth.gov/get-help/veterans

www.va.gov/homeless/resources.asp

www.pathintl.org/resources-education/
path-intl-equine-services-for-heroes

www.veteransfamiliesunited.org

www.taps.org

REFERENCES

National Institutes of Health. "Prevalence Estimates of Combat-Related PTSD: A Critical Review." www.ncbi.nlm.nih.gov/pmc/articles/PMC2891773/

U.S. Department of Veterans Affairs "Suicide Data Report, 2012." www.va.gov/opa/docs/Suicide-Data-Report-2012-final.pdf

RAND Center for Mental Health Policy Research. "Invisible Wounds of War: Psychological and Cognitive Injuries, Their Consequences, and Services to Assist Recovery." www.rand.org/content/dam/rand/pubs/monographs/2008/RAND-MG720.pdf

McGaugh, Scott. "Learning From America's Wars, Past and Present." *The San Diego Union Tribune.* 9/16/02 www.utsandiego.com/news/2012/sep/16/tp-learning-from-americas-wars-past-and-present/

U.S. Census Bureau. "A Snapshot of Our Nation's Veterans." Revised 10/28/14 www.census.gov/library/infographics/veterans.html

Lopez, Steve. "Kneeling again next to RFK." *Los Angeles Times* 11/21/10 www.articles.latimes/2010/nov/21/local/la-me-lopezcolumn-20101121.

"Editorial: VA Corruption a National Disgrace." *Las Vegas Review* Journal. 6/26/14 www.reviewjournal.com/opinion/editorial-va-corruption-national-disgrace

Steinbeck in Vietnam: Dispatches from the War, by John Steinbeck (Author), Thomas E. Barden (Editor)

THANKS
to these special people for their talent and support

Wendy Laister
Orla Clarke
Cody Alder
Denny Martin
Chris Merkle
Anna Judd
Cheryl Bennett
Brienne Mabry
Graham Bloem
Stefanie Bond

Molly Jenson
John Would
Nena Anderson
Deane Cote
Patrick McClory
Brian Young
Isaac Marr
Rami Jaffee
Caitlin Evanson
Daniel Mendez
Shannon Littrell
Jared Whitlock
Julie Steinbeiss

The veterans who shared their stories with me
and gave me eyes to see

And Jennifer

MUSIC CREDITS

Chariot
Written by Alex Woodard
Published by Woodshack Music (ASCAP)

East Texas Sky
Written by Alex Woodard
Published by Woodshack Music (ASCAP)

Fighter
Written by Alex Woodard
Published by Woodshack Music (ASCAP)

Black Ice
Written by Alex Woodard
Published by Woodshack Music (ASCAP)

Sing Me a Lullaby
Written by Alex Woodard and Molly Jenson
Published by Woodshack Music (ASCAP) / Wally Jay Music (ASCAP)

Breathe
Written by Alex Woodard and Molly Jenson
Published by Woodshack Music (ASCAP) / Wally Jay Music (ASCAP)

Stumble Into Light
Written by Alex Woodard and Molly Jenson
Published by Woodshack Music (ASCAP) / Wally Jay Music (ASCAP)

The Candle
Written by Alex Woodard
Published by Woodshack Music (ASCAP)

Crying Now
Written by Alex Woodard and Molly Jenson
Published by Woodshack Music (ASCAP) / Wally Jay Music (ASCAP)

Butterfly
Written by Alex Woodard
Published by Woodshack Music (ASCAP)

Maybe I'm A Rose
Written by Alex Woodard and Molly Jenson
Published by Woodshack Music (ASCAP) / Wally Jay Music (ASCAP)

Carry Me On
Written by Alex Woodard
Published by Woodshack Music (ASCAP)

Twilight
Written by Alex Woodard
Published by Woodshack Music (ASCAP)

Produced and recorded by John Would at Stanley Recordings
Mixed by Daniel Mendez and John Would
Mastered by Ed Brooks at RFI Mastering

* * *

ABOUT THE AUTHOR

When he's not surfing in a little beach town
north of San Diego, Alex lives with a big dog
and two bigger horses in the mountains of Idaho.

Please visit www.AlexWoodard.com
to learn more.

If you'd like to have your own
handwritten letter
considered for a song, please mail it to:

For The Sender
c/o Hay House
P.O. Box 5100
Carlsbad, CA 92018

While a song can't be written about every letter,
Alex does read them all. Please be sure to include
your contact information so we can reach out
to you if necessary.